The Torah Outlook on Marriage

by Rabbi Ezriel Tauber

Loneliness, confusion, silence—sadly and ironically, these are adjectives too often associated with marriage, the institution designed to unburden men and women of these conditions. Rather than a forum for the most noble emotions and aspirations, to many it is a prison of lost opportunity and failure.

- Are there marriages beyond hope? How do I find fulfillment in marriage?
- Do opposites really attract? What is in my hand to change and what is not?
- What is the purpose of marriage? Are there underlying principles to the numerous statements which the sages made relating to marriage?

To Become One is the real-life dialogue (fictionalized) of a couple seeking answers to these questions, as well as many others.

Genesis 2:24

"Therefore, a man leaves his father and mother, attaching to his wife for them *to become one.*" The secret to successful marriage is contained in this verse, and those who uncover the secret can improve their relationship immediately. In fact, that is how Rabbi Ezriel Tauber has been helping couples for over three decades who have sought his guidance. Contained in these pages, in dialogue form, is the formula he has used to help turn around marriages of all types, even ones that were unhappy for over twenty years!

His method is simple: Explain the root principles of the Torah ideal in order to empower others to grow into fulfilled individuals. By explaining the roots, he shows us how the branches, twigs, and leaves of our personal situations are really a single connected whole. All this makes *To Become One* a unique blend of the practical and the abstract. Read it. Enjoy it. And grow from it.

TO BECOME ONE

The Torah Outlook
on Marriage

by Rabbi Ezriel Tauber

Therefore a man leaves his father and mother, attaching to his wife, for them to become one.

Genesis 2:24

TO BECOME ONE

The Torah Outlook on Marriage

by
Rabbi Ezriel Tauber

with
Yaakov Astor

1st Edition 1990

2nd Edition
ISBN 1-878999-07-9
© Copyright 1991 by Shalheves.

Shalheves
P.O. Box 361
Monsey, N.Y. 10952
(914) 356-3515

". . . her flashes are like the flashes of fire, the flame of G-d (Shalheves Kah)."
(Shir HaShirim 8:6)

Printed in Israel

It was my great pleasure to receive the proofs of the second in line of the *"Hashkafa* Dialogue" series — namely "To Become One" — a comprehensive guide to *shalom bayit* by my close friend, Rabbi Ezriel Tauber, *shlita.*

Through my personal and continual close contact with Rabbi Tauber and his tremendous actions and deeds in supporting and disseminating Torah, and in particular his untiring and selfless efforts to help and rescue people in spiritual plight and distress, I have come to know him as a most successful and experienced marriage counselor, with a long list of saved marriages which had otherwise been on the brink of disintegration. His original Torah approach is at once profound and uplifting, yet practical and appropriate to our modern, contemporary society.

Rabbi Tauber has now recorded in his book some of his convincing arguments and sound and helpful advice to couples striving to rescue and correct their marriages. I can truly say that his approach propels what is usually considered the mundane, common-place and secular to great and lofty spiritual heights, transforming the Jewish home into a *Bait HaMikdash,* and family relations to service in the Holy of Holies. This true Torah *hashkafa,* based on Rabbinical sources, will surely help Torah-observant couples to purify and transcend their marital behaviour towards the lofty Torah-conception and standards, as a sublime service to the Creator.

I am sure many will derive benefit from the book and I offer Rabbi Tauber my best wishes and pray for his continual success in all his endeavors both spiritual and material. Amen!

Rabbi Yaakov Hillel
Rosh Yeshiva, Yeshivat Hevrat
Ahavat Shalom, Jerusalem

CONTENTS

ADAPTER'S FOREWORD: TIPS FOR READING THIS BOOK

With great joy we present the second volume of the *Hashkafa* Dialogue Series, entitled, "To Become One: The Torah Outlook on Marriage." Like the first volume, our purpose is to present authentic, penetrating Torah *hashkafa* (outlook) on the most relevant topics in a way that is both inspiring and enjoyable to read. For that reason our medium of choice has been the dialogue — a conversation between everyday people.

This book is not a novel. There are elements of literary expression and perhaps even drama which are by-products of the dialogue, however, our goal is not to engage the reader in narrative-like storytelling. Our goal is to teach Torah concepts. Real-life characters and natural conversation are some of the tools through which we presume to do that. Ultimately, this work is intended for the person with an interest in the content of the subject matter, who appreciates our attempt to make it more readable.

It is important to realize that the medium of dialogue has at least one advantage and one disadvantage. On one hand, it allows the reader to more easily finish the entire book from cover to cover. On the other hand, it is difficult to simply open to an interesting looking chapter or section and begin there. Not only will the reader be missing important background information about the characters and setting by doing so, but certain ideas and concepts are dependent on the fundamental principles laid down earlier in the dialogue.

Therefore, without first reading the entire book, a person is apt to draw conclusions based on insufficient knowledge. Questions may be raised which might otherwise be answered in an earlier or later part of the conversation. For this reason it is recommended that the book be read once cover to cover before focusing in on any particularly interesting theme. A light reading the first time around, we feel, is the best approach to benefitting from our work.

Another result of the relatively easy-to-read format in which this book is written in is the deceptive simplicity which results. The ideas in this book are by no means simple. They are merely written in this style which facilitates understanding on the part of a person with a limited background in Torah education, so that he can benefit from them; at the same time, the person with more developed understanding and insight can delve deeper and crystalize more sharply his or her thoughts on the topic at hand. For both types of readers, careful second, third and succeeding readings should produce newer and more satisfying insights. It is those insights which justify the format of this book.

Synopsis

To aid retention and understanding, the dialogue has been divided into chapters and sub-chapters. Glance through the Table of Contents to gain an idea about the general themes. For the interested reader, we also present the following short overview to the entire book:

Moshe and Shaina — This chapter introduces Moshe and Shaina, a couple who are experiencing marital difficulties. In addition to the nature of their particular (fictional) case, discussion about common myths and debilitating attitudes takes place, including the often-heard complaint that marital difficulties result because the husband and wife are so opposites.

The Marriage Perspective — As the title suggests, this chapter presents a perspective on the nature and goals of marriage. The need to grow as individuals, the true essence of giving and taking, the scheme of marriage in the design of creation — among other topics — are covered.

Deeper Insights — This section attempts to probe the depths of the Torah concept of oneness: how to attain it in a practical way, how the oneness of a couple is connected to the greater Oneness of the universe, and the place of the physical relationship in a marriage.

Woman — Modern society, for better or worse, has raised many issues concerning women. In the process, certain Torah practices and ideals, either out of misunderstanding or outright prejudice, have been maligned. Perhaps more damaging than the outrageous claims, are those subtle attitudes of the modern world which secretly infiltrate one's thinking. This has not only helped to further estrange Jews on the fringe of Torah observance, but has even sometimes threatened the well-being and marriages of those raised in Torah-observant homes. While not intended to serve as a comprehensive source for the issue, this chapter does attempt to identify the root principle underlying the Torah's concept of women in order to a) dispel misconceptions which for the most part only grew out of a fragmented, myopic understanding in the first place, and b) clarify statements and tenets which branch out from this root concept.

Common Problems — Practical Strategies — Some people like to open a book at the end. If you are one of them, this last chapter can almost stand on its own. It is devoted entirely to presenting practical strategies for overcoming some of the common marital difficulties which were set down in the first chapter. As such, if the middle chapters become too heavy, much can still be gained by skipping to this last chapter. (Of course, in order to be understood properly, the book needs to be read in its entirety.)

In addition, there are references, a glossary, appendices of statements from the Sages relevant to marriage, a recommended reading list, a tape list and information on Shalheves located in the back for your convenience. Please take advantage of them.

PREFACE

I am truly humbled and grateful to the Almighty for helping
me publish this volume on the Torah concept of marriage, the
second in our hashkafa series. And, again, I must begin by
expressing my debt of gratitude to the general public who
have attended the lectures upon which the material in this
book is based. For it is in the merit of those who attend my
lectures that Hashem graced me with the insights and original
thoughts which I delivered to them. Likewise, in their merit
has the material in this book been written. It is truly a
privilege to be able to deliver all these thoughts to them.

HAPPINESS. It is an elusive goal, especially in our times.
That makes it all the more strange to our ears, then, that the
Torah obligates us to serve G-d in a joyful manner. In fact,
failing to do so is counted against us, as it says, "[The bad
tidings will come upon you] because you did not serve G-d
with happiness and a good heart . . . " (*Devarim* 28:47).

The implication of this obligation is that happiness and
satisfaction are attainable for anyone and everyone.
Otherwise, how can G-d command us to serve Him with a
joyful heart? Perhaps, even more importantly, this obligation

teaches that happiness is not dependent on external circumstances. If it were, then how can G-d expect us to serve Him joyfully, plagued as we are with unhappy circumstances beyond our control? Therefore, even if the circumstances are beyond our control, happiness is in our hands.

The question is: What is the "magic formula" for attaining happiness?

The first answer is: Magic has nothing to do with it.

Many years of experience in counseling couples have taught me that *most* marital unhappiness results from a simple lack of understanding fundamental Torah principles: What is a man? What is a woman? Why is it necessary to be married? What can be accomplished through marriage? What does one lack without a proper marriage? Whenever I have been able to get across to a couple information on the fundamentals, their relationship has immediately improved.

The dynamic operating behind this is simple: Happiness is a function of knowledge. The Rambam (Maimonides) teaches that, "Love of G-d [and the ensuing satisfaction with life] comes only through knowing Him; in relation to the knowledge, so will be the love . . . Therefore, it is necessary to deepen one's knowledge of G-d as much as possible" (Laws of Repentance 10:6).

Serving G-d without understanding can turn everything into a chore. This is all the more so concerning the Divine service of living daily and intimately with our partner for life. To merely tolerate a spouse is an intolerable way to live, especially if we do not know why we should even bother. Conversely, perceiving even a small amount of the underlying reason behind G-d's plans turns even seemingly mundane chores into meaningful and satisfying actions.

The prophet Jeremiah said, "It is good for a person to carry a yoke from youth" (*Eichah* 3:27), to which the Sages ask: What yoke is referred to? The yoke of Torah and the yoke of marriage (*Eichah Rabbah* 3:9). Torah and marriage are compared to heavy loads, loads which weigh on a person's back over a long journey until he feels he is about to collapse. "Please," the person begs repeatedly, "relieve me of my load." However, the load cannot be removed; each person has been assigned a burden he must carry from the moment of birth until the last breath of life.

NEVERTHELESS, there is hope. Imagine someone could go over to the person under the load and tell him, "I can't remove the load from your back, but I can educate you about what you are carrying. You see, the baggage on your back is not a sack of valueless stones. In reality, you are carrying gems . . . diamonds. And, if you reach your destiny with this load, every diamond will be yours." Not only will this give the person strength, but perhaps he will even ask for a heavier load.

The intention of this book: to educate ourselves that every experience is a diamond, and that by overcoming our challenges, the diamonds will be ours. Through this approach, no matter how difficult the situation, we can all serve G-d "with happiness and a good heart."

The Sages tell us: "Working for a living and marriage are as difficult as splitting the Red Sea" (*Pesachim* 118a). At the miracle of the Red Sea, where Jew faced Egyptian, a person experienced one of two things: Either he saw G-d in all His majesty and glory or he drowned in the waters. These two opposite potentials are nowhere more self-evident than in our daily attempts to a) bring home an income and b) create a holy, stable, growth-oriented home environment.

Now, generally speaking, responsibility in a vital mission is apportioned between two people. For instance, every airline has a pilot and navigator. While the pilot actually flies the plane, the navigator makes sure it stays on course for its destination. The success of the flight is dependent upon the proper functioning of these two individuals.

Of course, there is a difference in their respective spheres of responsibility. A navigator's mistake is not catastrophic; the flight may be delayed and the passengers inconvenienced, but eventually they will reach their destination. However, a mistake by the pilot could indeed prove fatal.

So, too, with working for a living and marriage — the two vital missions which are as difficult as the splitting of the Red Sea. They have been divided between a husband and wife. The husband has been charged with the mission of venturing out into the world and bringing home an income; he is the pilot, in this respect, while his wife is the navigator. The primary responsibility of raising a family and building a home, on the other hand, has been put in the hands of the wife; there she is the pilot and her husband the navigator.

Only by working together in unison is it possible to fulfill the difficult and vital missions entrusted to each of us. Only in that way can we avoid the devastation of the surging waters all around and in fact create a manifestation of G-dliness in our lives which is comparable to the G-dliness manifest at the splitting of the Red Sea.

❧   ❧   ❧

It must be noted that everything expressed here falls only under the category of *hashkafa*, Torah perspective. No *halacha*, Torah law, should be derived from anything written herein without first consulting an authentic *Rav*.

Halacha and *hashkafa* differ in that the *halacha* cannot follow two viewpoints. In other words, although within the parameters of the *Shulchan Aruch* (the sourcebook of Torah law) the final *halacha* is not always uniform, the individual is obligated to follow the final decisions of his or her rabbi or community. An individual's personal *hashkafa*, on the other hand, is not so. The Ohr HaChaim states that, concerning *hashkafa*, not only are different interpretations of the same verse possible, but even interpretations which contradict each other are possible — in reality, he explains, each is a message for a different time and a different place.[1]

There are many ways to view identical situations. Each person, being a unique expression of the Divine image, has the potential to develop a legitimate, singular outlook on life. And even within one individual's singular outlook it is possible to simultaneously embrace multiple viewpoints, as *Chazal* (our Sages) say, "There are seventy faces to the Torah."

However, we do not have an open license. Impurities and distortions can easily creep into our thinking. Therefore, we must draw the substance of our life's outlook only from the well of living waters — Torah.

Hashkafa is like a jigsaw puzzle: it can only be made from the pieces which came in the box. Pieces from outside puzzles cannot be brought in. The building blocks of *hashkafa* are the statements of *Chazal*. Unlike physical jigsaw puzzles, however, *hashkafa* is multi-dimensional; the freedom of *hashkafa* is that two people can use identical statements of *Chazal,* and piece them together in unique ways — each according to the nature of his soul and the needs of his generation — while still expressing authentic words of the One Living G-d.

True *hashkafa* broadens our perspective of Torah; in no way does it alter the Torah. If it is authentic, it energizes all of one's life, enhancing one's ability to see the light in a dark situation, and even teaching one how to bask in it.

The *hashkafa* in my lectures and this book are fitted together only from the jigsaw known as *Chazal.* There is nothing that should be taken to imply anything which *Chazal* themselves opposed.

All the material used in this book, and, with the help of *Hashem,* in future books, has been said in public many times, including a three day audience with great Torah scholars in *Eretz Yisrael.* It was emphasized to these Torah giants how important their specific feedback was. This resulted in dozens of *haskamas,* approbations, which are available upon request.

On the same note, anyone who has questions and comments is encouraged to mail them to Shalheves. The only stipulation is that they be questions of *hashkafa,* not *halacha,* i.e., questions of Torah perspective, not Torah law.

I would like to give heartfelt thanks to all who have allowed me to continue with public lecturing. In particular, I want to thank the volunteers who run the Shalheves program in Monsey, and especially Mr. and Mrs. Gottlieb, who run the Shalheves program in Brooklyn. Also, I want to thank the writer of this booklet, Yaakov Astor. Due to his efforts, once more an otherwise complex subject has been made widely accessible without detracting from its depth and beauty.

Last, being the most precious, if not for the dedicated support of my dear family, none of this would be possible. May it be *Hashem's* will that we merit to continue with strength and see the Redemption, speedily, in our days.

Ezriel Tauber

TO
BECOME
ONE

CHAPTER 1

MOSHE AND SHAINA

Depositing a lone passenger, the bus whirred away, leaving in its wake a swirling puff of exhaust smoke and fumes.

Shaina was lost.

She was sure that the bus just departed had been the wrong connection and had taken her far from her stop. It was not the safest looking neighborhood, and she sensed a wave of panic about to crash into her. In fact, she felt herself falling apart at the seams.

Grabbing hold of her emotions, she told herself to calm down and find someone to help direct her to her destination. Suddenly, her eyes fell upon the figure of another Torah-observant woman walking by. Her heart thumping with relief, she stopped the woman, calmly told her where she needed to go, and asked if she could help her find her way.

WOMAN: Come with me. I'm going in that general direction myself.

SHAINA: Oh, you are? Thank you. I appreciate your help a lot, but you don't really have to take me all the way. Just tell me how to get there and I'll go myself.

WOMAN: No. I will gladly take you. I too would feel nervous if I were in strange surroundings.

SHAINA: Nervous? Does it show?

WOMAN: Well, you do seem a little ruffled.

SHAINA: I am, but I was hoping it wouldn't show. (Pause.) Why is it so hard for me? Why does it seem like G-d has abandoned me?

WOMAN: Abandoned you? Those are very harsh words.

SHAINA: It just seems that life is getting more impossible every day.

WOMAN: From your words I can guess that you are not upset only because you are in an unfamiliar neighborhood.

SHAINA: Yes, but maybe I have already said more than I should. I don't want to complain. I have to be thankful for what I have. (She begins crying, and then regains control of herself.)

WOMAN: We have to be thankful for what we have, but we also have to know what we have; then we really have something to be thankful for.

SHAINA: I guess I don't feel like I have anything.

WOMAN: That is very sad, then, especially since you have so much.

SHAINA: What do you mean?

WOMAN: You're alive. That may sound simplistic, but at the very least you have life.

SHAINA: I may have life, but it doesn't feel like I am living.

WOMAN: As long as you have life, though, you can rest assured that there is something *Hashem* wants from you. Every situation is from Him; some seem better, and some seem worse, but in every situation there is something we can do or think which can have a profound influence above and below, whether we see it or not.

SHAINA: But what good is my life if my marriage is falling apart?

WOMAN: (Pause.) Ah, now I understand why you're so upset. I'm sorry if I sounded insensitive.

SHAINA: No, you didn't. I appreciate your words.

WOMAN: I really feel for you very deeply. I was in a similar position myself not too long ago.

SHAINA: You were?

WOMAN: Yes. And I can tell you that what I just said is one hundred percent true: Every situation can bring about something great. Even a completely hopeless marriage, if there is such a thing, has hidden within it some spiritual pot of gold which only that situation can cash in.

SHAINA: You sound like someone who has a lot of wisdom.

WOMAN: I learned the hard way — through experience. Plus, I happen to have a special teacher. Trust me, though, no situation is unproductive. I doubt that your marriage is hopeless.

SHAINA: I suppose that if my situation were really hopeless my husband and I wouldn't be going to a marriage counselor. In fact, that's what I'm doing here; I'm going to meet my husband at the counselor's office.

WOMAN: That's something to feel positive about.

SHAINA: Yes, I have heard that this man has helped a lot of people.

WOMAN: You're not talking about Rabbi___, by chance, are you?

SHAINA: Yes (with surprise). Do you know him?

WOMAN: He is the teacher I was telling you about. He can help you get a whole new perspective on things; he helped me. And, by the way, here is his office.

SHAINA: What? So close? But the bus — I was sure I took the wrong bus.

WOMAN: You may have been sure, but *Hashem* was sure you took the right bus. He led you to where you were supposed to go, and He happened to put me right there to greet you. You see? There is no situation, no matter how desperate, which is not part of some higher plan — if only we can see it from that perspective. Listen to me, I'm even beginning to sound like the Rabbi.

I really have to run now, but tell him the story. I'm sure he will appreciate it. So long, and good luck.

Opposites

Although the sun was beginning to set, light flooded in through the large window of the rabbi's office giving it a well-lit, spacious aura. Across from the desk where he sat were two chairs — one occupied by Shaina, and the other empty. Shaina tapped her finger nervously on the armrest.

SHAINA: I knew he wouldn't show up. He doesn't take it seriously.

RABBI: Give him time. He probably got caught up in traffic.

SHAINA: It's so typical. We never connect. We are such opposites. That's why I think our marriage doesn't work.

RABBI: Being opposites is more proof that your marriage was meant to work. The Torah says very clearly, "It is not good being man alone, I will make a helper opposite him."[2] In other words, how will this helper help? Through being the opposite of him.

Of course, the secret for success in marriage is learning how to deal with (and ultimately harness) the opposition. However, the more opposite two people are of each other, the greater is their marriage when they learn how to fuse themselves into one.

SHAINA: Should I be happy, then, that we are such opposites?

RABBI: Yes. Of course, generally speaking, when we go out and look for a partner in marriage we should look for someone who seems to be similar. To do otherwise would risk bringing upon ourselves a difficult situation which we have no right to create of our own doing. However, no matter how much we try to fight it, we cannot outsmart *Hashem*. He will match us up with the one with whom we can accomplish that which we were put in the world for; and that means someone who is not the same as us, someone who is often directly the opposite of us.

SHAINA: What you are saying makes sense, but it doesn't really make my situation any easier.

RABBI: It doesn't lessen the degree to which you have to work to make your marriage successful, but it can help make the work less burdensome. Nevertheless, you are right: Marriage is not easy. In fact, let me illustrate to you just how difficult a situation can be.

A couple once came into my office. From the outside it was hard to imagine how two such young people raised in homes permeated by *shalom bayis* —

harmony — could complain so bitterly about each other. And the more I looked into it the more I was able to confirm that each of them was raised in a truly harmonious home.

You should know, though, that homes such as the ones where these two were raised do not come about by chance. And many times the harmony in these homes cannot be credited to both parents. When I inquired further I found out, indeed, that only one parent in each home was responsible for the harmony.

In family A, the man was a nervous wreck with a quick temper. It was not really his fault. He was a survivor of the holocaust. His father, also a survivor of the holocaust, beat him regularly; his teachers used to beat him. What could one expect from the poor man? The woman, on the other hand, was a *tzedeykus,* a truly righteous soul, who understood her husband perfectly.

She knew that the harmony of the house depended upon having everything prepared when he got home. When he stepped into the house, she could look at his face and know exactly the right words to greet him with. Before he ever had a chance to blow up she knew how to squelch anything that would lead to discord. Meanwhile, the children grew up not suspecting how deficient their father really was. She would always tell them, "Your father is the greatest *talmid chacham,*" or "he is the greatest charity giver."

I happened to know that he is the opposite of that description, but the mother convinced the children otherwise. It was she who built that beautiful home.

In family B the situation was just the reverse. The father was a *tzaddik*, while the mother was . . . how shall I put it? I cannot even describe how unsettled this woman was. She never knew what she wanted, always screaming for and demanding the opposite of what was offered. Despite it all, her husband never walked into the house empty-handed. Everything could be upside-down; it didn't matter to him. He would bring home take-out food, set the table and say, "Honey, look how nicely you set the table." As a result, the children grew up blind to the undercurrent in the home.

Now, the *shadchan* — the match-maker — looked at these two families and saw a beautiful boy from harmonious family A and a beautiful girl from harmonious family B. The boy, inheriting all the insensitivity of his father, walked under the wedding canopy expecting his wife to be everything he saw in his mother, the *tzedeykus*. The girl, meanwhile, stepped under the canopy — a replica of her mother the screamer. She expected her husband to be a *tzaddik* like her father. Not surprisingly, problems started in the *yichud* room!

Could I really blame them? Each party came to me demanding his/her rights, expecting the other to be just like the righteous parent. I sat there thinking, "Master of the World, what do you want me to do here? They are both right."

SHAINA: What did you do?

RABBI: I asked them to tell me who their match-maker was. Both of them immediately started cursing the person who set them up. I quieted them, and asked if they could tell me who their real match-maker was. They had to admit, of course, that it was *Hashem*.

"If you have complaints," I told them, "then first scream to *Hashem*. Don't yell at the match-maker. Don't yell at your father or mother. And don't yell at your husband or wife. Both of you are innocent. Turn to *Hashem* and ask Him why he put you in this situation. And if you ask," I told them, "He will answer."

SHAINA: Was there an answer?

RABBI: Of course. Each case is different, and I am not going to go into the details of that particular one, but, in general, even then I realized that these two were unpolished diamonds. They had to stick it out.

I don't know if you know the diamond line, but cheap diamonds are very easy to polish. A real diamond is rough; it's black, it's hard, it has knots, and if you were not a maven you would not even recognize that it was a diamond. However, a professional looking at such a stone would say, "Wow! Let me put it on the wheel right away."

On the wheel the stone screeches, screams, yells, and wants to jump off, but it is precisely this polishing and cutting process which brings out the gem. Such a diamond can start out at ten carats, and when the jeweler finishes it may be two carats, or even only one carat. But what a precious gem! There was a lot of rough in this couple, yet it was obvious that if they submitted to the process — if they stayed glued to the wheel — they could have a beautiful marriage, far superior to those who always had things easy.

The intercom buzzed. "There is a man here who says he has an appointment with you."

"Show him in."

A few seconds later, the door opened and in walked Moshe, a little out of breath as if he had been running. Taking the seat next to his wife, he caught his breath and explained:

MOSHE: I'm sorry for being late. I got a very important call at the last moment, and then by the time I finally left it was rush hour, and then I had trouble finding this place. I know that my wife doesn't think that I take this seriously enough, but I really planned to get here on time.

RABBI: Nobody suspected you of anything. I'm glad you could make it. Can I offer you a cup of coffee or perhaps something else to drink?

MOSHE: No thanks.

RABBI: Okay, then let me allow you to catch your breath while I bring you up to date a little on what we have been discussing.

Basically, we haven't gotten into any specifics, but I was just explaining to your wife the common fallacy that if two people seem to be opposites it is a sign that they are not compatible, and that their marriage is doomed to failure. Nothing could be further from the truth. *Hashem* created husband and wife as opposites; the more opposite and difficult a spouse is, the greater it is when they achieve unity.

Marriage is like a wind-up watch. The spring, which is wound very tightly, is held back by a pin which allows the spring to unwind a single tick at a time. If the pin is removed the spring unwinds and expends itself in a second. The spring and pin perform opposite functions, but together — and only together — they create time. In marriage, too, often one partner — sometimes the man, sometimes the woman — is the energy while the other works in opposition, but the tension creates a perfect whole.

Marriages begin to falter not because the partners are natural opposites of each other, but because the couple stops putting in effort to overcome and harness the differences between them; they stop putting in effort toward the union, and they stop putting in the effort to improve their individual selves. *Hashem* made

it such that harmony in marriage has to be worked for;
only then can the couple accomplish everything for
which they were created.

MOSHE: But isn't it true that some people, through their
actions, forfeit their *bashert,* the person they were
originally meant to marry?[3]

RABBI: Yes. So what?

MOSHE: If that is true, then how can there be harmony
in a marriage which is not with one's *bashert?*

RABBI: First, if you are implying that you may not have
married your *bashert* — the partner who at conception
heaven decreed was intended for you — I have to
inform you that you have no way of definitely knowing
that for sure. And no one can tell you otherwise.

Second, while it is true that according to the *Talmud*
a person's actions may result in his marrying a partner
other than his *bashert,* successful marriage is not
dependent upon marrying one's *bashert.* A marriage
between two such ideally matched people, unworked
upon, can be miserable; conversely, a marriage
between a couple that does not have that status of
bashert can work out wonderfully.[4]

Third, despite your best efforts, *Hashem* makes sure
that you come to the conclusion to marry the partner
whom He deems best suited for your ultimate needs.
Whether it is your *bashert* or any other type of spouse,
Hashem is always the match-maker.

MOSHE: If so, then how come the Torah has a *mitzvah*

to divorce?

RABBI: Because people have free will to make a situation work or not work.

MOSHE: But doesn't *Hashem* know beforehand if it will work?

RABBI: Yes, but His reasons for doing so are none of our business. All we know is that just as *Hashem* puts couples together, sometimes He wants them to separate. Don't take that to mean, however, that on your own you can determine whether *Hashem* wants you to divorce or not.

MOSHE: But what if there is no peace in the home?

RABBI: It is true that when a couple can no longer live together peacefully they must divorce. Nevertheless, the couple is too biased to come to that decision by themselves. They have to go to an objective third party, who understands both, and who gets them to try everything. If afterwards they are told that there does not seem to be any hope, then and only then is it possible to conclude that perhaps the couple is better off separating.

MOSHE: I'm not saying I want a divorce, but why subject two people to all that extra torment when they can make a clean break and start all over fresh?

RABBI: Because there is no such thing as a clean break.

MOSHE: Then how come many second marriages succeed where first ones don't?

RABBI: First, when second marriages are successful it is

because the couple works three or four times as hard to make sure they do not have a repeat of the first marriage. Therefore, to begin with, rather than considering divorce a person should consider putting into his present marriage one-third or one-quarter of the amount of energy he would have to expend in order to make a second marriage successful.

Second, in addition to the extra effort, second marriages are successful because both parties go at their work with a new attitude. There is a joke — not such a good one, I admit — about a couple who divorces, and right after it becomes official the husband turns to his former wife and proposes. The rabbi, stunned, says to him, "But you just divorced her?!" Confidently, the man answers, "She doesn't make a good first wife; but she would make a good second wife." The point is that a lot depends on your attitude. Rather than starting a second marriage with a new attitude, learn to develop a fresh attitude now.

The bottom line is that divorce is like an amputation. Would you go to a doctor and tell him to amputate a leg because the pain is unbearable? No. Amputation is a last resort; hopefully he can cure the pain without such extreme measures. And then, if in fact there is no other recourse but to amputate, can it ever be said that the person is happy that he has to live with the trauma of an amputated limb? Divorce, even when justified, is no less devastating and traumatic. The

Talmud says that the altar of *Hashem* sheds tears whenever a divorce has to occur.[5]

MOSHE: But living in pain can be so hard.

RABBI: Yes, but being in a difficult situation is not enough of a reason to divorce. So, it is hard. Life is hard. It is not going to last more than seventy or eighty years.

MOSHE: But I don't want to spend my whole life suffering if I can avoid it, and neither does Shaina.

RABBI: That, I assume, is why both of you are here: to find out how to make your marriage work better.

SHAINA: Yes, rabbi, I want to learn how to make it work; I don't want to give up.

RABBI: Good. You should both realize that every marriage is literally a match made in heaven, even second, third, and fourth marriages. Once we accept that fact, then we have to look within ourselves to begin to improve the situation.

MOSHE: Excuse me one second, but why do I have to look to myself? I didn't do anything wrong.

RABBI: No one is saying you did, but we are all imperfect human beings. We all have faults. All I meant to say is that we have to focus on improving our part; when that happens, then the rest will begin to fall into place.

MOSHE: But maybe it is her fault.

RABBI: Anything is possible. However, it's easy to look at the other person and say he or she is wrong. When it comes to other people we are experts, but if there's a blemish on the tip of our own nose we don't see it. Maybe you're the one at fault.

MOSHE: Maybe.

RABBI: But let's not think in terms of one party being right or wrong. Usually both sides contribute to the difficulties. If *Hashem* puts us in a situation, then we have to work it through. That is all I am trying to say. I have counseled a lot of couples and have found that anything is possible if they have not given up.

MOSHE: How long have you been counseling?

RABBI: Thirty-two years.

MOSHE: Thirty-two years?

RABBI: Yes, and I still remember the first couple I worked with. In fact, I'm still working with them on a daily basis.

MOSHE: Then, you must not have been too successful with them.

RABBI: On the contrary, they are growing and growing all the time.

MOSHE: How do you know that with certainty?

RABBI: Because that couple is my wife and I. There is no comparison between the appreciation I had for my wife then versus what I have for her now. No comparison. Every single day produces something positive in our marriage; we have never let it grow stagnant.

MOSHE: Every single day? How is that possible?

RABBI: Because our differences do not let it grow stagnant. Once you become numb to the fact that a man and a woman are opposites — that you and your spouse are individuals, each with your own quirks — then your marriage is dead.

Do you think that young couples are the only ones where the pangs of being opposite are felt? Older couples are no less opposite than younger ones. In fact, as the couple matures, if they have not let themselves become numb, they grow even more aware of the differences. By then, though, they have hopefully developed the tools of give and take necessary to overcome and harness their differences.

MOSHE: With all due respect, rabbi, I don't see how someone can be aware that the person he lives with is his opposite, and at the same time live peacefully with her.

RABBI: Let's look into it, then: Say you went through a computer agency to find your spouse and filled out an application with 1,000 characteristics of the perfect mate. After a week the computer came up with three nearly perfect candidates. Then you dwindled the three down to one. Do you really think you would be happy?

MOSHE: Why not?

RABBI: First, because there would be no challenges to confront and overcome; the lack of friction and stimulation would ultimately make you more unhappy. Second, the truth is that you wouldn't even get what you asked for. You see, people who fall in love at first sight also think the other person is nearly perfect — as if an applicant with the exact 1,000 characteristics they asked for suddenly appeared. However, after getting to know the person they begin to see that the "application" was "just a piece of paper." In reality, the person projected certain qualities to the outside world, while on the inside was entirely different.

Hashem does the same with us: He shows us someone who appears to coincide with our "application request," but when you get down to it is not at all what you expected. And *Boruch Hashem* for that. In the end, you will love the person more so for being your opposite and for having faults.

MOSHE: I admit that I'm not perfect, but can you really love someone if you see his/her faults?

RABBI: Yes, and I'll prove it to you? Who in this world loves you the most?

MOSHE: The most? I would have to say my mother and father.

RABBI: Good. And who would you say knows your shortcomings more than anyone else? Obviously, your mother and father. They were there when you were fighting with your siblings, when you didn't clean up after yourself, and when you got into trouble in school. They know all your faults inside-out. Yet no one loves you more. Therefore, seeing faults in others has nothing to do with the amount of love you can feel for them.

Your wife is not perfect. And you are not perfect. You may in fact be complete opposites. In spite of it all, *Hashem* put you together, and there is no reason to assume that He does not want you to stay together.

The Pyramid

SHAINA: If that's the case, rabbi, then what is the problem with our marriage?

RABBI: There is no problem with your marriage. The marriage is fine. The problem in your or anyone else's marriage is with the individuals: he doesn't know who he is; she doesn't know what is demanded from her; they don't know what they have to dedicate their lives to. Become better, more fulfilled individuals, and your marriage will automatically improve.

SHAINA: That makes sense.

RABBI: On this note, now is a good time to explain to you something about the way I work. My methods are not like those of any marriage counselor. Generally, marriage counselors and psychologists attempt to bring couples together. It sounds good, but the problem is that the two people as they are may not want to come together; the closer they get, the more they repel each other. My goal is to bring you together, but by first getting you into a groove where you are growing as individuals in the way *Hashem* intended when He gave us His Torah.

Let me illustrate it this way: Imagine a pyramid; at the foot of it, standing at opposite corners, are two people. Rather than getting them to walk directly toward each other, my aim is to get each one to walk up his or her side of the pyramid. The closer each gets to the top, naturally the closer they get to each other.

If both of you are willing to leave behind the part of you which is on the ground, you can begin to create a genuine closeness, a closeness based on a mutual revamping of who you are for the sake of reaching the common point between you. My goal is to help you reach the common point.

MOSHE: In real terms, what is the common point?

RABBI: The Torah ideal of oneness is the point of the pyramid. When oneness is reached, then the *Shechinah,* the Divine Presence, is said to rest on the couple.[6] The *Shechinah* is a synonym for the feeling of holiness, purity, spirituality — whatever you want to call it. It is the ultimate state of being, and experiencing that state continually is the purpose and goal of marriage.

This idea is conceptualized in the Hebrew words for man and woman.[7] Man — *ish* (spelled *aleph, yud, shin*) — and woman — *ishah* (spelled *aleph, shin, hey*) — are three letter words which share two common letters (*aleph* and *shin*) and one letter unique to each (the *yud* of *ish,* and the *hey* of *ishah*). The letter unique to each represents a distinctive spiritual component which marriage is designed to mesh together as one. And when these unique letters — the *yud* and *hey* — are brought together they spell *Hashem*'s name. The lesson is: The job of man and woman is to utilize their unique letters of holiness, raising and reuniting them at the peak of the pyramid.

On the other hand, what happens if these letters are unused or abused? In that event, all that remains is the *aleph* and *shin* of *ish* plus the same *aleph* and *shin* of *ishah*; *aleph* and *shin* spell *aish*, fire. In other words, husband and wife lacking the goal of spiritual union, like two consuming fires, will destroy each other.

My goal is to teach you what it means to raise and properly utilize your unique spiritual components, so you can turn the fire of your relationship into the fuel for attaining oneness. First, however, each of you must realize that the Torah has a set of unique and distinct requirements for the man as well as a set of unique and distinct requirements for the woman. By fulfilling your individual requirements, your striving for closeness will not repel each other. On the contrary, if both of you make a commitment to grow and change yourselves and become Torah-imbued individuals you will become "one flesh," to use the Torah's terminology.

A One-Sided Pyramid

MOSHE: Excuse me, rabbi, but did you say there was a coffee machine here?

RABBI: Yes. Down the hall.

MOSHE: I'll be right back, then. (He exits.)

SHAINA: Rabbi, to return to your analogy of the pyramid, what if one party is reluctant to climb up the pyramid? Can oneness be reached even then?

RABBI: Yes. It would be much easier and nicer if both worked equally, nevertheless, if only one side makes an investment — a double investment — the oneness is possible. You see, even if one person were to remain at the bottom of the pyramid, as long as the other one reaches the top a link is created to the one at the bottom. In a spiritual sense, this means that the souls have come together even though, in a physical sense, the two bodies are still far apart. Of course, the credit for the accomplishment of oneness would be given only to the one who worked for it. Even so, the positive by-products will accrue to all members of the family.

SHAINA: It seems unfair, though. Why would *Hashem* pair up a couple where one works and the other doesn't?

RABBI: Perhaps I can answer your question by relating the story of a person who came to complain to the holy Arizal about his wife.

"Whatever I want," the man said, "my wife does the

opposite. It has become unbearable. Should I divorce her?"

The Arizal, with his deep mystical vision, said, "This is your *tikun,* this is the way you can 'repair' a fault in your spiritual self. In a previous existence the situation was reversed: you were the bad one."

The man not only accepted his words, but changed his entire outlook. He realized that it was worthwhile to suffer because, as he saw it now, every time his wife tried to annoy him another crease in his soul was straightened out. And she did continue trying to annoy him. The worse she became, however, the happier he was. Try as she may, he would only smile, tell her thank you, shower her with gifts, and become even more loving.

Finally, she broke down and asked what changed in him. He told her the words of the Arizal, and how her opposition was a *tikun* for his soul.

"What!" she screamed. "I'm giving you a *tikun,* a way of repairing yourself?! Forget it." With that she became the most loving and cooperative wife. Anything he wanted she gave him.

A few days later the husband began panicking. He returned to the Arizal and complained, "You see, my wife is so bad that she doesn't want to give me the *tikun* which I need."

The Arizal calmed him and said, "You received your *tikun* already. She changed her behavior toward you not because of her own design, but because in heaven they saw how you accepted your wife's opposition with genuine love and thanks. This was the exact repair your soul needed."

Only he reached the peak of the pyramid, so to speak, and yet it affected both parties. Thus, here is a perfect example involving a case of spiritual reunion where the physical bodies are not even aware that the reunion took place. Furthermore, this story provides is one answer to the question as to why *Hashem* creates an outwardly unfair situation, namely: Even in an unbalanced relationship suffering frequently serves as a *tikun*.

SHAINA: How does a person know whether difficulties with a spouse are a *tikun* or just suffering for nothing?

RABBI: There is no such thing as suffering for nothing if a *talmid chacham* tells you that the best thing is for the marriage to continue.

The thing to focus on is that we are not in control of our spouse's actions; we are only in control of our own selves. Each member of every couple needs to take it upon him or her self to improve what is in his or her hands to improve, and not demand more. Fulfill your responsibilities to *Hashem* and leave the rest to Him. One way or another, sooner or later, things will straighten out.

Seeing With Two Eyes

Moshe returns.

MOSHE: Rabbi, I was just thinking about what you said
and I like it, however, practically speaking, what can
you do for us so that we can reach your goal of
oneness?

RABBI: First, Moshe, it is not my image of fulfilled
individuals or my vision of oneness in a marriage that
I am advocating. It is only the Torah's image of human
and marital perfection that I am trying to promote.
Second, I can't really do anything for you. All I can do
is help you find meaning for yourselves in the Torah's
ideals.

MOSHE: And how do you propose to do that?

RABBI: Through explaining the teachings of our Sages,
and by impressing upon you how their words form the
steps to the peak of that pyramid. Therefore, after
finishing tonight, I will give you a sheet of sayings from
the Sages[8] — to you, Moshe, the sheet will contain
those statements designed specially for the man, and
for you, Shaina, the sheet will have those statements
designed specially for the woman. In addition I will
give you a sheet containing statements concerning
marriage which are common to both men and women.

By committing yourselves to their words both of you
will move forward up your individual steps. I have
seldom seen a bad marriage when two people began

to fulfill their personal duties. If a man does what he has to do and a woman does what she has to do the marriage will work. Not knowing or not listening to our Sages pulls you apart.

SHAINA: What you are saying, then, is that you feel we basically have the means to a good marriage; you just want to help us utilize those means.

RABBI: Exactly.

MOSHE: I just don't understand what you will do differently from anyone else.

RABBI: My goal for our time together now is to give you a new pair of glasses with which to look at the words of the Sages, to help you see the larger picture so that those words will not seem like isolated fragments. Once you understand and appreciate the underlying unity behind these statements, then both of you can review and study the sheets, and grow from them the way they were meant to nourish you. You should study the sheets every day till they become part of you. If you have any questions I will gladly answer them.

You see, my underlying assumption, Moshe, is that fulfillment in marriage, as fulfillment in anything, depends mostly on internal factors, and, generally speaking, is a result of seeing the larger picture. Seeing the larger picture taps into the power source of happiness — living with a sense of purpose.

Many couples come to me and tell me that they do not see "eye to eye."

"The problem is," I tell them, "that you are only looking with one eye. But *Hashem* created you with two eyes — take a look at things in the larger context with a little depth and perspective."

A Jew who understands who he is and what marriage can do for him will deal with the frustrations of marriage far differently and more successfully than one who only fulfills the Torah out of habit, like a robot.

The same is true for single people. I was asked recently to speak to such a group. I told them that marriage is actually looking for your other half. "Why do you have difficulty finding your other half?" I asked them. "Because you have not found the first half. You have to first know who you are, what your destiny is, where you are going. Then you will know what you are missing, what you have to get, and where to get it. Marriage is designed to replace that which you do not have."

Similarly, many marital problems are compounded by the fact that people have an underdeveloped Torah perspective. Their problem is not lack of human potential, but lack of knowledge. Fill in the gaps, broaden the scope, and the particulars begin to fall into place.

From experience I can tell you that I have seen couples who were married for twenty years and who did not have a good day in their lives, but once they began to understand what *Hashem* wanted from them and committed themselves to live accordingly they became a new couple.

Therefore, I feel it is essential that I take the time right now to convey to you some basics about the Torah's concept of the marital relationship, as well as some of the fundamental Torah ideas related to that subject.

SHAINA: Okay.

MOSHE: All right. I'm agreeable. Where do we start?

RABBI: Let's start in the beginning.

CHAPTER 2

THE MARRIAGE PERSPECTIVE

The Five Levels of Creation

In the Torah's record of the six days of creation four elements are described: rocks (inanimate objects), plants, animals, and man. The description of the creation of man concludes the fourth of the four elements, as it says: "Let us make man in our image, like our form; and he will rule over the fish of the sea, the birds of the heaven, the animals," etc.[9]

Now, the statement "Let us make man" is unusual. All the commentators ask why the statement is in the plural. Whom was *Hashem* speaking to? The Ramban states that *Hashem* was speaking to the earth.[10] In fact, he explains, all the raw material of creation was actually produced in the first instance, with the first word, *Beraishis* — "In the beginning". During the ensuing six days of creation *Hashem* pulled out of the ground, so to speak, each of the elements. Therefore, *Hashem* said, "Let the *earth* sprout vegetation" "Let the *earth* bring forth animals" etc. Similarly, writes the Ramban, when *Hashem* said, "Let us make man" he was addressing the earth to bring forth man.

The earth "obeyed" and man was formed. Still and all, even with his intellect and speech, man was only one of the four elements; he possessed only a *nefesh behamis,* a body-oriented, animalistic soul. He was the dominant being of the physical creation, but he was nothing more than a dominant, speaking being who existed within the four basic elements of the physical creation.

However, as the earth brought forth man, the Ramban explains, *Hashem* — and *Hashem* alone — added a new dimension: the *tzelem Elokim*, the Divine image. Therefore, right after the verse "Let us make man" the Torah says: "And *Hashem* created man in *His* image . . ." This second verse tells us that man with "His image," with *tzelem Elokim*, is a fifth element of creation, the creation called *Yisroel oved Hashem*, Israel who serves G-d.[11]

Thus, in addition to man's animalistic soul — his *nefesh* — *Hashem* gave man a Divine soul — the *neshama* — as the Torah says: "And He blew into him a ***nishmas*** *chaim* (an eternal soul)."[12]

MOSHE: Intellectually, I've heard this before, but frankly, what does it mean to have a *neshama*? We have to eat. We have to sleep. We don't fly around. Does this *tzelem Elokim* manifest itself practically in our lives?

RABBI: Of course. To properly understand how the image of *Hashem* is manifest in our lives, first we have to understand a little about what *Hashem* is. With our limited intellects we can understand at least two things about *Hashem*: He has absolute free will and He creates. In other words, He is not forced to do anything in any way, and He can even make something out of nothing. First and foremost, then, the *tzelem Elokim* — the G-dly potential in man — empowers us with free choice.

In actuality, it was the creation of the *neshama* which gave physical man free will because with it he now had two souls: *Neshamos ani osisi*, "souls (plural) I made"[13] *Hashem* tells us. With the *nefesh behamis* — the animal soul — and the *neshama* — the Divine soul — man now had the ability to choose to associate with either one or the other.

MOSHE: Practically speaking, though, what does it mean to choose to associate with the physical or the spiritual? Choose what?

RABBI: Simply put, it means whether one's orientation is toward giving or taking.

SHAINA: That's interesting.

RABBI: In order to really understand that statement, though, first I have to provide a little background information. The Arizal four centuries ago, and later Rabbi Moshe Chaim Luzzatto,[14] asked: Why did *Hashem* create the world? Of course, we cannot presume to know *Hashem*'s true motives, however, these unique Torah masters were able to present us with a glimpse of an answer to this perplexing question. They explain that since *Hashem* is good, and *the nature of good is to want to give good to another*, He created an "other" in order to have an object upon which to bestow this good. Creation is that object.

Thus, creation was an act of *chesed*, altruism. *Hashem* does not need anything from it. Nevertheless, because He *is* good, He desired an object upon which to bestow His goodness. Thus, the Creator created the world in order to give.

Now, since *Hashem* created the world in order to give, perforce, then, the world has built in needs which only *Hashem* fulfills. Plants need sunlight, animals need food, etc. And nothing needs more than man — the ultimate creation, the ultimate receiver.

You can see this clearly in newborns. A human child is totally helpless and defenseless, more so than any animal. At birth all it can do is scream to get its needs fulfilled. It is a high level receiver. This is because man is at the top of the physical creation. Nevertheless, as a part of the physical creation, even though he dominates the world, man can be nothing more than a receiver, nothing more than a taker.

However, *Hashem* — the Ultimate Giver — wanted to give man the ultimate gift, and therefore, as we said, He gave him the Divine image, an actual deposit of Himself. Ironically, though — and here's the point — this part of *Hashem* Himself in man, this *tzelem Elokim*, is *the capacity to give*, the capacity to be more than just a mere receiver like the physical elements.

Through giving, man on the fourth level — physical man — becomes spiritual. He promotes himself to the fifth level of creation. In fact, through giving, man even becomes Creator-like, the second characteristic of *Hashem* which I mentioned, because the spirit is his essential self, and he creates this self every time he imitates *Hashem* through the act of giving. In reality, then, when we give, we create ourselves — we create in our selves a part of *Hashem*. *Hashem* gives us a creation on the fourth level; our job is to give back to Him a creation on the fifth level.

Oved Hashem

SHAINA: What you are saying is very beautiful, rabbi. I always knew it was a Jewish thing to give, but I didn't realize that giving was actually the idea of choosing to associate with *tzelem Elokim*.

RABBI: Yes, genuine giving is the highest form of imitating *Hashem*. Taking, on the other hand, weighs down the spirit. The important thing to remember is: Man is cast into a situation where he has an instinct to take; at the same time, *Hashem* gave man the opportunity and ability to become a creation with *tzelem Elokim*, a giver. Thus, this life, as an arena for free will, offers us two paths: You either become *Hashem*-like and a giver, or you remain a taker. There is no middle ground. One's heart is dedicated either to giving or to taking.[15]

MOSHE: That sounds extreme. How is it possible not to want to take? Even according to what you said we have a physical body that wants to take.

RABBI: Yes, there is no question that a human has to take; the body was created to receive. However, there are two types of taking: taking for the purpose of taking and taking for the purpose of giving. A selfish person will also give; however, he gives only so that he can get back twice as much. To him taking is an end in itself and giving is the means.

In order to genuinely associate with the *tzelem Elokim*, however, we must give just as *Hashem* gives, i.e. even without getting anything in return. We must view giving as an end in itself. When we take, we must take only to be able to give back or only for the purpose of allowing the other to give. In this way we can orient everything we do toward giving.

SHAINA: Can you show me a real-life situation about the second example, where one can take in order to allow the other to give?

RABBI: Yes. Imagine a parent buys a toy for his child. A couple of days later, the parent peeks in the child's room and sees him thoroughly enjoying the toy. Every moment the child derives pleasure from the toy, the parent is reaping his own pleasure. Through the child's taking — using the toy as it was meant to be used — he is giving the parent pleasure.

This is what happens in our relationship to *Hashem*. *Hashem*, by definition, needs nothing, and, therefore, there is nothing we — His creations — can give Him. The one thing we can do, however, is accept His giving. In that respect the more we accept *Hashem*'s gifts and derive pleasure from them, the more pleasure we give Him. You could say that our receiving becomes an act of giving.

This is the concept of being an *Oved Hashem*, a servant of G-d. A true servant of *Hashem* takes from Him because he knows that *Hashem* (if we were permitted to say it) enjoys giving — like the parent who gives his child a toy. An *Oved Hashem* accepts and even yearns for the pleasure he derives from the world (as long as it is within the specifications explained in *Hashem*'s Torah. To take things which the Torah forbids indicates clearly that he takes to satisfy himself and not in order to give to *Hashem*). The *Oved*

Hashem thinks to himself before benefiting from the world: Is this only to satisfy my desire or to allow *Hashem* to give? In this way, he serves *Hashem* continually, twenty-four hours a day. Even his sleeping is a service to *Hashem*, since he does so only in order to gather strength to serve *Hashem* better the next day.

Abraham was the highest example of a human becoming a total giver. He dedicated his entire life to giving, as anyone who has delved into the details of his life knows. Finally, *Hashem* gave him the ultimate test and opportunity to become a total giver: sacrificing his son, his only son, the one whom he had waited 100 years to have.

Abraham understood that just as *Hashem* gave him a gift, so, too, he had to prove that he was not just taking for his own benefit, but only in order to allow *Hashem* to give. The world needed to see that he did not require children to fulfill himself, but only to allow *Hashem* the pleasure of being able to give. He did so by carrying out the command to sacrifice his son to *Hashem* with the same excitement and enthusiasm that he felt when he was given his son. This proved that none of his actions were dependent on receiving. He became the complete *Oved Hashem*, the complete giver.

And that is why Abraham is the beginning of the Jewish nation. He is the essence of what it means to

be a Jew by representing the ability of man to give
Hashem the opportunity and pleasure to give. If one
purifies his intentions in this manner, nothing is higher.

MOSHE: But why only a Jew? When a gentile takes, why
isn't that the same form of giving to *Hashem*?

RABBI: A Jew is unique in creation by virtue of the fact
that *Hashem* commanded him to fulfill the Torah;
fulfilling the Torah is the Jew's way of giving to
Hashem because in the Torah it is reiterated time and
again how *Hashem* equates carrying out His commands
— His *mitzvos* — with receiving blessing from Him.
Therefore, whenever a Jew fulfills the *mitzvos* with
pure intentions he gives *Hashem* the opportunity to
give him blessing. And nothing pleases *Hashem* more.
Through performing *mitzvos* we become the
consummate givers to *Hashem*.

This, by the way, allows us to explain the statement
sachar mitzvah mitzvah,[16] in a new light. Normally, we
understand it to mean: "The reward of a *mitzvah* is
(the opportunity to perform another) *mitzvah.*" Now,
however, we can read it: "(Accepting and reaping
enjoyment from) the reward of a *mitzvah* is the
mitzvah (a righteous act in itself, because our enjoying
Hashem's blessing is giving *Hashem* pleasure)." The
act of the *mitzvah* — putting leather boxes on our
head and arm or strings on a four-cornered garment
— is not the real essence of the *mitzvah*; it is the
reward we get for *t'fillen, tzitzis,* and the other

commandments, which is the essence of the *mitzvah,* because getting that reward means that *Hashem* is giving. Making oneself over into a creation who allows *Hashem* to give is what Abraham our forefather taught us all about.

Love and Marriage

MOSHE: But wasn't Abraham's greatness in his giving to human beings?

RABBI: Yes. That is no contradiction to what we just said, though: By perfecting himself in the arena of giving to human beings, Abraham was able to become the prototype giver to *Hashem.* And now we can begin to talk about marriage, because Abraham's ability to give to human beings started with his ability to give selflessly to his wife, Sarah.[17]

You see, marriage, on a person to person level, is the forum for giving. Nothing else matches this opportunity to transform oneself into a giver, into a creation with *tzelem Elokim.* Thus, the Torah says: "And *Hashem* created the man in *His image*; in the image of *Hashem* He created him; *male and female* He created them."[18] Wherever male and female are mentioned *tzelem Elokim* is mentioned.[19] This teaches that the relationship between a man and a woman is the most fertile soil for breeding *tzelem Elokim.*

MOSHE: But weren't animals — who do not have *tzelem*

Elokim — also created male and female?

RABBI: Yes, but the Torah does not find it important enough to mention; the distinction of male and female is stated only where man is mentioned and always in connection with *tzelem Elokim.*

SHAINA: Why is that?

RABBI: Because animals have no concept of marriage; they only follow their instincts. They have no concept of giving for the sake of creating G-dliness within themselves. At best, it is only giving to get something in return.

MOSHE: Let's be honest, though, rabbi: Human beings also give only because they get something in return, right?

RABBI: No.

MOSHE: If it is not because we get something in return, then what makes a person want to give? Is it unreasonable to expect to get something back in return?

RABBI: The only thing you should expect to "get" from giving is the pleasure of knowing that you were able to give.

SHAINA: Can you repeat that?

RABBI: Yes. The only thing you should expect to get from giving is the pleasure of knowing that you were able to give. *Giving is an end itself*, a pleasure in its own right. And the feeling of pleasure from giving comes from the *tzelem Elokim* in each of us. In some people, admittedly, the pleasure associated with giving is buried deep down, but like coal it can be ignited and fanned; it is very important to always fan to keep the embers glowing.

In any event, true giving is giving for its own sake, or giving to bring out the *tzelem Elokim* in you. If you give for these reasons, then you will be worthy to always receive pleasure from the giving itself.

SHAINA: Can you define this pleasure more tangibly for me?

RABBI: Yes. That pleasure is called love. Love is a by-product of giving. The more you focus on the giving, the more you love. The more you focus on anything else, the more likely it is that the love will dissipate.

SHAINA: Isn't it the other way around? The more you love, the more you give.

RABBI: That may be true as well, however, the essence of love is in the giving. The Hebrew word for love, *ahavah,* attests to that: the middle two letters of the four letter word spell *hav,* meaning, to give.[20] The love that exists between a man and a woman centers on one thing — giving.

MOSHE: What about people who fall in love at first sight? They haven't had the opportunity to give to each other.

RABBI: What many people call love today, more often than not, is nothing other than self-love. You probably heard the story of the person eating fish, who when asked why he ate the fish so hungrily replied, "Because I love fish."

"It's not the fish you love," he was told, "but yourself. If you were thinking of the fish you would feed it and change its water. You wouldn't slice it up, fry it, and eat it. Rather, you love yourself, and to satisfy yourself you cook fish and eat them."

What many people call love today is really just another fish story. They say in the same way, "I love my house; I love my Volvo; I love my spouse." Is that fair? Can love toward a spouse be the same as love toward material objects? The answer is yes if you love your spouse on the condition that he/she gives you something in return. In that case, however, you would actually be talking about self-love.

SHAINA: Is self-love bad? Aren't we supposed to love ourselves?

RABBI: True, the Torah says, "Love your friend as you love yourself,"[21] implying that you have to love yourself, however, the question is: What do we love ourselves for? For our body or our soul? If it is for our body and the things we consume, then it is a selfish love, a love which emanates from the urge to take. If, on the other hand, we love ourselves for our soul and the urge to give, then it is true love. Love, as the word is often used today, is not always a good thing. The bottom line is: If you give, you love; if you take, you love yourself.

MOSHE: But everyone is a taker.

RABBI: Everyone has a natural inclination to take. It is no surprise, then, that marriages often get off to shaky starts. However, the whole point of marriage is to become a giver, to exploit your most valuable natural resource — your *tzelem Elokim*.

MOSHE: If we have a *tzelem Elokim*, then, what makes giving and marriage so difficult?

RABBI: Because along with the *tzelem Elokim* — the *neshama* — we possess an animal soul — the *nefesh behamis*. Or, to explain it more simply, we possess both a soul and a body. The body's pleasure is in taking. It is the part of man similar to the animals; it is from one of the four elements which are only capable of receiving, as we explained. The body is our animal. It only wants to take.

If fulfillment of the body — pure taking — is the only motivation of getting married, then marriage is little more than a business contract. "I need you and you need me," couples with this mentality say (in various ways and degrees). "Therefore, let us form a company. The company will be called Mr. and Mrs. Company which will live under such and such roof. Whatever I need, you will give me. Whatever you need, I will give you." These people act like two takers who sign a contract to service each other. If they find different partners who service them better, from whom they can take more, they break the contract.

But how much is there, after all, that one can take? A generation or two ago, the needs of the body could suffice for thirty to fifty years worth of taking. Today young couples start falling apart after the honeymoon. State-of-the-art advertising agencies have perfected the art of stimulating the body's needs to the point that it cannot find fulfillment fast enough. After a year or two, if that long, nothing is left of the relationship between the average couple indoctrinated with the outlook that fulfillment means fulfillment of the body's needs.

A marriage based on fulfilling the soul's needs, though, is just the opposite. It builds as time goes on. The giving perpetuates itself, and leads to ever heightening levels of pleasure. Yes, there is taking, but soul-based taking is only for the sake of giving. The reverse is true for the body, where one's giving is a tool in order to take.

Body and soul operate like a horse and rider; first, the horse has to be broken-in in order to harness it. Then it becomes a vehicle for use. If it controls us, we are tossed about and are in for a rough ride.

Success in marriage occurs when both partners conquer and harness their bodies' needs, when each one transforms all of his or her acts into acts of giving despite the pull to make everything an act of taking. It is when husband and wife give to and take from each other purely with the intention of satisfying the other that they transform themselves into pure givers, beings on the fifth level of creation.

MOSHE: It just sounds like a very high ideal.

RABBI: I am not saying it's easy. Each of us has conflicting desires. Our soul-need — the need to give — is commingled with our body-need — the desire to take. If *Hashem* wanted us to live as celibates and ascetics, people who mortify the physical, it might be easier. But He does not. He wants us to marry and take part in the world, because only where there is so much at stake can so much be gained.

It is very hard, especially when you are young, to separate your need to give from your need to be given satisfaction. The body's needs compete with the soul's needs. This is what makes marriage so challenging. However, this challenge also explains why fulfillment of self can only occur through marriage.

MOSHE: But aren't there couples who are happy without all this challenge and difficulty?

RABBI: There are many who appear happy in marriage, but their happiness is superficial and can be toppled by even a slight change in external circumstances. The truth is that many of these couples have not even taken up the challenge of trying to harness the body's desires; they have not even begun fulfilling their purpose in life. If life is not for growth through challenge, then what value is there in it?

MOSHE: I'm not saying I ever expected it to be easy, but

sometimes it seems impossible.

RABBI: It is a very difficult job, indeed. However, at the very least we should know what our goal is, what it is we have to focus on. And when we fail — and a lot of times we do fail — we should be able to admit in a private moment that we were not true to our higher self. If we do not admit that, then we are not being honest with ourselves and are not creating a frame of mind where we can improve.

Let me tell you of a personal incident, which I suppose is the most effective way of impressing upon you that successful marriage means harnessing and sometimes even sacrificing your body's needs to satisfy the needs of your spouse.

More than twenty years ago, during a particularly busy period in my life, I had to be on the road all day. I would come home around seven o'clock, exhausted and tense. The second I stepped in the door, I was flooded with complaints from my family: this one wouldn't share with that one, and that child is not helping out, etc. I would tell them, "Listen, I have to go lie down for fifteen minutes, and then I will take your complaints."

Hearing this my wife would say, "I've been waiting all day for you, and now you want me to wait an extra fifteen minutes!"

She was right, of course.

MOSHE: You were right, too, though.

SHAINA: What did you do?

RABBI: According to Jewish law, a man has to love his wife as himself, *and take care of her needs even more than his own.*[22] The woman's responsibility is only to love her husband as she loves herself. It was my responsibility to give in.

I reflected on my predicament and it suddenly dawned on me that a large part of my problem was that I would finish my lunch before two o'clock. By seven o'clock I was starving. My body's needs were crying to be met. This made it extremely difficult for me to be patient, and pay attention to the needs of others. I resolved that the next day I would make sure to save a piece of cake and a cup of coffee for later. Before getting home I pulled my car onto the shoulder of the highway and closed my eyes for fifteen minutes; then I took the coffee and cake, and went home.

MOSHE: Did it work?

RABBI: Yes. By the time I got home I had no difficulty listening to all the problems.

Generally, the most trying situations in life determine whether a person is devoted to giving or taking. It is at precisely those times that we must be strong enough to give. Those are the most difficult tests in life, but they are also the situations which produce the most, turning mundane people into reflections of *Hashem.*

To attain the goal of becoming "one flesh" we have to be one hundred percent prepared to give up something of ourselves. You have to get married, but if you expect to become a giver — if you really expect to bring out the *tzelem Elokim* in yourself — your marriage has to be a training ground for becoming truly selfless. Nothing less will transform you into a *tzelem Elokim*. It is not magic, however. Two people have to work on themselves individually and in unison.

Joy, Blessing, Good and Torah

MOSHE: There are many ways to give. How come you say that you can only become a giver through marriage?

RABBI: Because every other giving situation is almost invariably tainted with the possibility that you do it for ulterior motives. If you give donations, perhaps it is to be honored; if you go out to save the world, perhaps it is because you have visions of grandeur for yourself. Marriage, though, occurs mostly in the private sector; no one except your spouse knows how much you really give of yourself. Plus, the opportunities for giving in a marriage are constant, and often subtle. Above all, marriage is not easy; you have to continually overcome yourself in order to give, even when you are tense and don't feel like it.

MOSHE: Nevertheless, you make it sound like everything is dependent upon it.

RABBI: Everything is. If a man fails in his home, he will

fail on the outside, whether his "outside" is in the *yeshiva* or the business world. The *Talmud* says: "One who lives without a wife possesses no joy, blessing, good or Torah."[23] This also applies to married couples who do not attain the Torah ideal in marriage — they live without joy, blessing, good and Torah; they have no pleasure in whatever it is that they do.

SHAINA: Rabbi, this is exactly the way I have been feeling. Although a lot of things have fallen into place for us, there is still this constant feeling that something vital is missing.

RABBI: The reason for that is that the home is the place where everything begins. Let me tell you about an old acquaintance I bumped into not long ago.[24] I asked how he was doing.

He shook his head, "Not too well."

"What's wrong," I asked.

"I have three big problems," he said. "First, my business is going nowhere, and it's been that way for a long time despite all my best efforts. I am falling deeper and deeper into debt every day.

"Second, I just received a phone call from the *yeshiva* where my son is learning, and the principal informed me that he recommends my son attend a different *yeshiva* high school next year. The principal was gracious, but I could gather from his words that my son is making so much trouble, and they are so sick and tired of him, that they want to kick him out.

"Third," he continued, "my *shalom bayis* is shot. When I come home every night I'm on edge — I'm a bag of nerves — and all my wife and I do is yell at each other. The situation in the home couldn't be worse."

"Listen," I told him, "from what you are telling me, it sounds like you don't have three problems — you have one: *shalom bayis,* lack of peace and tranquility in the home. The Sages tell us that a person should be very careful with the honor of his wife because blessing only comes into the household of a man through his wife.[25] Therefore, instead of trying so hard at your business, why not start putting that same effort into your home life?"

"Furthermore," I continued, "the problem with your son is also rooted in lack of domestic tranquility. If your home is a place of calm, where everyone is considerate and speaks politely to each other, then your children will also be calm; when they go to school they will be relaxed enough to listen to the teacher. However, when your son comes home from school, he comes into this pressure cooker where the tension is so great he is afraid to say or do anything. What can the poor kid do? When he goes off to school he is finally free to let off steam.

"Nothing is more important than *shalom bayis* for the wholesome development of yourself and your children," I stressed to him, "Nothing! If there is no money in your house, you can get over it; if your apartment is too small, you will get over it; if you can't afford to send the kids to camp, you will get over it; if you can't afford a bicycle for your kid, he'll get over it — whatever might be lacking is not a major problem. However, if there is no *shalom bayis,* the children, in addition to the parents, will be scarred."

Being The Man Alone

MOSHE: Let's be honest, though, rabbi, you make it sound as if the relationship is the most important part of being married. The real purpose of marriage is to have children. That's the *mitzvah* which the Torah talks about.

RABBI: Nothing could be further from the truth, Moshe. Marriage is not just a vehicle for having children. Yes, we must have children; that is an independent commandment in the Torah. In addition, though, there is a *mitzvah* to be married. The proof is that if the couple have no children, or are incapable of having children, or are so old that they can no longer have children, they each have a *mitzvah* to be married.

I once paid a *shiva* call to a great, revered rabbi whose wife passed away. They had been married more than forty years. During the week of mourning he asked me to come by once the grieving period was over. I had the privilege of working with him in the past on certain projects, so naturally I thought he had another such project in mind.

I came to him as he had asked, and he told me, "The Torah says, *Lo tov heos haAdam levado*, 'It is not good being man alone.'[26] The Zohar explains that a man is literally 'not good' when he is alone. I do not want to be considered 'not good.' Therefore, since you have the opportunity to travel around a lot," he said, "will you please keep an eye open for me concerning a *shidduch*, a wife."

I was shocked. Here was an elderly man who had lived with his wife in harmony for more than forty years. What personal benefit could he gain from remarrying? He had children and disciples ready to attend him. Yet, he saw marriage not as a means of fulfilling a personal need; it was a requirement of the Torah. It was part of perfecting himself and becoming an absolute giver. Only marriage could remove him from the status of "not good" and put him in the status of "good."

A man alone is not just someone who lacks good. He is someone in a state of being which is called "not good." Why is he not good? Because he does not have the means to truly give, to convert himself into a *tzelem Elokim*. Marriage, in its highest sense, is an end in itself. It is the forum for learning how to give for the sake of becoming a G-dly being. That makes it a basic requirement of life, not just a means to some other goal.

CHAPTER 3

DEEPER INSIGHTS

Spiritual Sharks

MOSHE: Rabbi, let's say a person doesn't count or consider becoming a G-dly being as his number one priority? What I mean is let's say he's basically happy with who he is and wants to keep the Torah, but he doesn't entertain visions of himself becoming this G-dly being, as you put it. He is not so spiritual.

RABBI: There is really no choice in the matter, Moshe. One who does not busy himself with growing spiritually is busying himself with dying spiritually.[27] *Hashem* put us in a world where there is an inherent gravity of the spirit. Like a shark, which must swim constantly to pass water over its gills in order to remain alive, we, too, must move and grow constantly to keep ourselves spiritually alive.

That is why *Hashem* tells us, "I put before you life and death, a blessing and a curse — choose life."[28] He doesn't say "don't choose death." That is because death is not a choice; it is man's natural state if he does not exert himself to attain life. Therefore, we have no choice but to make the attempt to launch ourselves past the gravity of our natural atmosphere into the world of the spirit.

MOSHE: But why should I pursue a lifestyle which is too high for me to maintain?

RABBI: Firstly, you don't know if it is too high for you to maintain until you really try it. Secondly, even if you have setbacks, "A person does not acquire true wisdom in the words of Torah, unless he first stumbles in them."[29] Torah, life, business, marriage — anything of true value — can only be acquired through first experiencing and then overcoming failure. Therefore, we have no alternative but to at least make the attempt to reach the stars, disregarding our fears of failure.

MOSHE: Easier said than done.

RABBI: True. Nevertheless, it is also "easier done when said." The more we repeat it over and over again, the easier it becomes to live up to it. We have no choice but to live up to the Torah ideal. One who does not, succumbs to spiritual death.

MOSHE: But I know that I am not on that level.

RABBI: You, as you are now, may not be on that level, but how do you know that you won't be once you start growing? After all, if you have really grown, then you have become in some way a new self who your earlier self could not have fully grasped. So, you don't know if you can or can't be on that level. Plus, we have a principle that if a person seeks to perfect himself here below, heaven helps him from above.[30]

MOSHE: I guess you are making sense.

RABBI: There is no choice in the matter. You and your wife have to begin seriously working on the Torah ideal of oneness.

Mystery and Oneness

MOSHE: What exactly do you mean by oneness?

RABBI: Let me relate an incident to you which is told of the *tzaddik*, Reb Aryeh Levine. One time his wife injured her foot. They visited the doctor together and Reb Aryeh said, "Doctor, my wife's foot is hurting *us*." This was no slip of the tongue or dramatized response. He had genuinely become one with his wife; her pain was his. This is the level of unity which is meant when the Torah says that husband and wife will become "one flesh." Each partner has to reach this level of oneness where there is no "I" and "you".

MOSHE: But I'm not an Aryeh Levine.

RABBI: Nevertheless, you and your wife are capable of achieving a comparable oneness.

MOSHE: How do you know that?

RABBI: Because of the way *Hashem* created you. You see, in truth, every husband and wife are a single soul temporarily divided in half and placed into two bodies.

SHAINA: Can you say that again?

RABBI: Yes, every husband and wife are in reality a single soul.

MOSHE: I'm confused: Aren't husband and wife two individual entities?

RABBI: They are only half-entities.

MOSHE: But I am a complete body.

RABBI: Right, and if you consider your body your self, then you are no better off than an animal. The purpose of marriage, and the reason two people are really attracted to each other, is to reunite these two half souls. Let me explain it further. It is a key concept, and one that is very important for you to be able to visualize.

MOSHE: Okay.

RABBI: Adam and Chava (Eve) serve as the model for this concept. Let's examine the account of their creation.

Originally, Adam and Chava were a single entity which contained both male and female characteristics. This is what the Torah means when it says, "Male and female He created them."[31] In other words, they were opposite poles of a single soul. From that one soul, which was placed in the body called Adam, *Hashem* removed the female half of the soul and put it into a body called woman. In actuality, though, they were half-souls; husband and wife are one entity.[32]

Every couple today has the same task as Adam and Chava; they are really one soul with male and female characteristics housed in two bodies who must (and were given a natural urge to) fuse back into one. Moshe, I notice hesitation on your face.

MOSHE: That's because you seem to be talking about it literally.

RABBI: I am. To prove it to you, let me show you how this idea finds itself in other areas of Torah thought as well.

I don't know if you are aware, but in the mystical writings there is reference to something called a storehouse of souls. This is a place where the souls are "stored" before coming into this world. Now, why should *Hashem* need a storage area for souls? Can't He just place the soul directly into the body? A book called *Shefa Tal* written several centuries ago asked and answered that question.

The Shefa Tal writes that the storehouse for souls acts as a way-station for whole souls destined to be divided and then sent down — one half at a time — into a body. In other words, the entire concept of a storehouse for souls is founded on the understanding that originally *Hashem* created one soul possessing both male and female characteristics which is destined to be divided and put into two separate bodies. Since the bodies will not be created at the same time — husband and wife can be born years apart — the half-soul which remains needs a place to wait. The storehouse of souls is where it waits. The storehouse, then, serves two functions: First, it is the place where the whole soul rejoices as one, and second it is a way-station for the remaining half-soul which waits to be dispatched and sent down into a body.

The *Talmud* tells us: "Forty days before the formation of the fetus, a voice proclaims, 'This soul is destined to marry so-and-so.'"[33] Once born into this world, the half-souls are separated for many years until one day they instinctively start seeking each other out. The attraction they actually feel is rooted in each of these half-soul's yearning to reunite with the other half.

SHAINA: Why go through this elaborate process of creating a single soul, dividing it in half, all only in order for it to reunite again? Why not just create independent souls and give them a commandment to reunite?

RABBI: Because the original oneness leaves the deep impression in each half that they are really one. It creates a potential for love and unity even greater than

the potential oneness between siblings or relatives.
"Therefore, a man should leave his father and mother,
attaching to his wife for them to become one." The
potential oneness between a husband and wife is
unparalleled in life.

The idea that man and woman are one soul explains
other statements of the Sages as well: Under the
marriage canopy, for instance, and during the festive
week of *sheva berachos* that follows, the newlyweds are
blessed: "Rejoice. Rejoice, good friends with each
other . . ." Good friends? We know that the Sages
were careful with every word of every blessing they
composed. At such an early stage in their relationship
how can this couple be called "good friends"?

The answer is explained in the ensuing words of the
blessing: ". . . just as *Hashem* caused you to rejoice in
the Garden of Eden before." What is meant by
"before"? Before when? The answer is: "before" they
were divided and came down to the world; "before"
the one-half was dispatched from the storehouse of
souls. That's why they can be called good friends even
if their marriage was arranged, and they saw each
other only once or twice before the actual wedding.

Along the same line of thought: The first time we
say a blessing for the creation of our selves,
surprisingly, is under the wedding canopy. Only then
do we say the blessing concluded *Yotzair haAdam,* "the
Creator of man." Why not say that blessing at our bar-

mitzvah or some other time? The Ishbitzer Rebbe writes that the reason is because the Divine soul is not complete until the marriage. Until then they are only two halves.

Moshe, I see from your expression that you are still not satisfied. Perhaps I am speaking on too high of a level.

MOSHE: No. I think I understand it well enough, and in fact I like discussing these ideas on a higher level. However, are you saying that a husband and wife, as nothing more than half-souls, have no individuality independent of each other?

RABBI: No. The heart and brain of a person are part of a single entity, nevertheless, the heart serves a function different from that of the brain. All I mean to say is that there is a level of unity which every couple is capable of achieving where they live, act, and think in unison with each other — where it can be said that they fuse into one. And when that happens they are able to look back upon certain difficulties they may have had in their struggle to become one and say, "How could I ever have underestimated how vital marriage is to becoming a whole person? How could I not have seen the pleasure inherent in becoming one with my spouse?"

The Ultimate Oneness

The bottom line is that oneness is tangible. As I told you earlier: "One who lives without a wife (i.e., a marriage where the couple has not attained the level of "one flesh") lives without joy, blessing, good and Torah." It is something you can know whether you have attained it or not.

Of course, even to speak of oneness as an emotion or pleasure that encompasses all emotions and pleasures actually does injustice to the idea. A marriage is actually a reflection of larger things.

SHAINA: What type of larger things?

RABBI: *Hashem* gave power into our hands to cause separation or bring unity to the entire universe. This means that your and every other couple's striving to become one is not just an isolated event. It is plugged into the happenings of the entire universe. A husband and wife in the privacy of their home can create a cosmic unity that no other area of life can reproduce.

MOSHE: That's a very heavy statement.

SHAINA: Can you elaborate on this?

RABBI: Yes. Marriage is a miniature replica of the universe. The universe is nothing more than a stage for the unfolding drama of *Hashem* and creation striving to become one.

Man, the pinnacle of creation — and the righteous man, the pinnacle of mankind — is *Hashem*'s partner in creation. To draw on the analogy of King Solomon,

Israel is the bride of *Hashem*. In fact, this is the theme of Song of Songs. On the surface it appears to be a love ballad between a man and woman. In actuality, it is a declaration in the most profound and beautiful terms of the love between *Hashem* and Israel.

MOSHE: Don't you mean between *Hashem* and creation?

RABBI: No. Israel is the pinnacle of creation. You see, Israel is descended from Abraham. Abraham, in turn, was the first absolutely righteous man, as I told you earlier.[34] As the first absolutely righteous man he became the focal point of creation.

In fact, that is why the written Torah does not go into detail about the creation of the universe; neither does it elaborate much on the lives of Adam and Noah. Only when it reaches Abraham does it start relating information in detail. That is because things which are most beloved are paid attention to even down to the smallest details. Therefore, an entire planet's worth of otherwise monumental history is not worthy of note in the face of a single individual who goes to the root of the purpose of this world — who strives to imitate *Hashem* in a world which seeks to deny Him. Abraham was that person, as the Zohar points out for us: Don't read, "These are the generations of heaven and earth 'when He created them (*b'hebaram*).' Rather, rearrange the letters of the last word and read it, 'for Abraham' — the heavens and the earth were created 'for Abraham'.[35]

From Abraham, the first absolutely righteous man, the Torah details the lives of Isaac, Jacob and his offspring, the first absolutely righteous family. After a lifetime of struggles, Jacob, the Torah informs us, merited receiving the name Israel. That is the main idea set down in the Book of Genesis.

The Book of Exodus goes into detail over how the family of Israel was molded into the nation of Israel, an entity worthy of special attention if for no other reason than their status as descendants of Abraham, Isaac and Jacob. In the "iron furnace" of the Egyptian exile they were purified and molded until the point when they were ready to stand at Mount Sinai to receive *Hashem*'s Torah. The revelation at Mount Sinai was the most momentous event not only in Jewish history, but in world history. In fact, it is referred to as the wedding of Israel to *Hashem*.

SHAINA: What exactly was so special about the giving of the Torah at Mount Sinai among the many events in history?

RABBI: Because it was the fruition of *Hashem*'s intention in creating the world.

MOSHE: What intention was that?

RABBI: To become a giver. When Israel received the Torah, she became the true focus of His giving — the quintessential receiver. As I told you earlier, creation is the action of *Hashem* separating a part of Himself in order make a receiver which allowed Him to give.

Before then, so to speak, He was alone; there was nothing upon which to manifest His goodness. When He created the world He transformed Himself into a giver.

Hashem, though, the ultimate Giver, wanted to bestow the ultimate gift — the *tzelem Elokim*, that part of Himself upon the worthy recipient. To do that He needed to give man free will so that man could earn the gift. Therefore, *Hashem* waited twenty generations for the one absolutely righteous person to step forward and utilize his free will to transform himself into an absolute giver despite overwhelming adversity. For this singularly righteous individual *Hashem* waited because this individual would allow *Hashem*'s love to shower forth. Abraham, as we said, was that person. In essence, he was the one who allowed *Hashem* to become a giver. Therefore, *Hashem* calls him "Abraham, my beloved."[36]

Israel, the national entity, was charged with the mission to become just like Abraham, who did everything only for *Hashem*'s pleasure. As we said, every pleasure which he felt, he felt in order to appreciate *Hashem*'s giving; everything that he took, he took in order to give. Therefore, the more he took, the more he gave *Hashem*.

The Dynamics of Oneness

With this introduction, now we can understand the secret of attaining oneness between a man and woman.

SHAINA: Please explain.

RABBI: Israel, as *Hashem*'s bride, plays the receiving role, the female role, in the interaction.[37] The more Israel takes (as a means to giving *Hashem* pleasure, so to speak) the more *Hashem* gives. The greater the genuine give and take, the more oneness is generated.

This is the way a man and woman need to relate to each other in order to cultivate unity and oneness between themselves. Generally speaking, the more the woman receives, the more fulfilled she is. And the hungrier to receive she is, the more the man enjoys the act of giving.

The worst thing a wife can do to her husband is reject that which he has to offer. If he wants to give, but she says, "I don't need you," it is as if she sticks a dagger in him. Her way to self-improvement is to learn to take — to receive — with the intention of satisfying her husband, even if she happens not to need it. That type of receiving is, in reality, giving.

SHAINA: Could that include a wife who asks for guidance even though she feels deep down that she doesn't need the advice?

RABBI: Yes. Now, please don't conclude that I am saying she has to deny herself. There is nothing wrong with looking to have one's natural desires fulfilled in the proper context. Quite the contrary, if the receiver genuinely feels satisfied with the receiving, the giver's pleasure in giving is increased. She must utilize those natural desires with the intention of making her husband's act of giving more pleasurable. To the best of her ability, she even has to create opportunities for her husband to give.

And, just as a woman's deepest desire is to receive and is optimally fulfilled when she can receive, so, too, the man's deepest desire is to give and is fulfilled most by giving. Of course, just as she must receive for the sake of satisfying him, he must give in order to satisfy her.

MOSHE: Can you supply me with a real-life example?

RABBI: Yes. For instance, a couple came to me arguing over a present. He wanted to buy his wife a $400 piece of jewelry. She, however, told him that she really wanted a particular pocketbook for $100. He bought her the jewelry anyway because he wanted to give the bigger, more prestigious present. When he saw her sour expression he felt rejected. They got into an argument and came to me.

I explained to him that his job is to give in order to please his wife, and if she wanted the pocketbook he should have looked to satisfy her. Fulfilling his own need to buy the more expensive gift was misplaced generosity. A husband has to constantly ask himself, "How can I fulfill my *wife's* desire?"

The secret for success in marriage is intimated in the Torah's statement: "Therefore, a man should leave his father and mother, attaching to his wife for them to become one." There are three partners in the birth of a human: the man, the woman, and *Hashem*.[38] The man and the woman supply the body, while *Hashem* supplies the soul. The Torah answers the following question for us: How can a man become one with his wife? He has "to leave his mother and father", i.e., he has to abandon the physical when approaching his wife; he has to abandon the inclination to be a receiver on the fourth level of creation, the inclination to demand that his own needs be fulfilled before anything else.

SHAINA: Why is the Torah only addressing the man in that verse?

RABBI: Because man, as the giver, has the responsibility to initiate the cycle of give-and-take. If he refrains from giving, there is no chance for the woman to perform her part.

The perfect relationship is when both husband and wife have the maximum desire for each other; he has the maximum desire to give, and she has the maximum desire to receive. This in fact was *Hashem*'s design in creating Adam alone.

MOSHE: That's interesting. What do you mean by that?

RABBI: When *Hashem* said, "Let the earth bring forth animals," the whole world filled up with animals.

When *Hashem* said, "Let the earth bring forth vegetation," the whole world filled up with vegetation. Everything was created complete and in multiples — everything except Adam, man; he was created a single entity and incomplete, as it says, "It is not good being man alone."

From the beginning, therefore, man possessed an inescapable potential for loneliness. His feelings of loneliness were aroused further when *Hashem* made all the creatures of the world pass before him. When Adam saw that there was no creature like him he knew he was indeed alone.

MOSHE: Why did *Hashem* do that to Adam?

RABBI: Because he wanted to draw out from him the maximum desire for Chava. Only after doing so did *Hashem* "cause him to fall into a deep sleep" and create Chava. You see, *the giver only feels satisfaction to the degree that the receiver is capable of appreciating the gift.* Only after seeing how all the animals could not fulfill him was it possible for Adam to awaken and fully appreciate that Chava was his completion; she was his partner, the only one for whom his deep-seated urge to give was meant.

Therefore, the desire of the giver to give and the taker to take creates oneness. In the ultimate sense, that is the dynamic operating between *Hashem* and Israel. That is why at the moment of marriage under the wedding canopy *Hashem* is blessed as the One

"Who sanctifies His people Israel through betrothal and marriage." In other words, the spiritual closeness which is produced by the natural give-and-take a couple generate in the privacy of their own lives sanctifies all Israel, and from there it spreads and sanctifies the entire creation and universe.

To Become One

MOSHE: Rabbi, where does the physical relationship fit in the Torah's perspective?

RABBI: I'm glad you asked, because understanding the answer to that is really the culmination of everything we have been discussing. The physical is the *means* to the goal of soul reunion; it acts as the cement of the union, securing and tightening the bond between two half-souls which are dedicated to giving.

Intimacy is glue. Like glue it works only in the proper context, in the proper quantity, with the proper quality — not more and not less. If you want to glue together a broken vase, for example, before you even apply the glue, the surface has to be clean. Otherwise, when the glue dries, the outline of the crack will be discernable. In the same way, the purer the intentions of a husband and wife in living with each other — the cleaner the surface — the less noticeable it will be that there was ever a crack.

Next, after making sure the surface is clean, you

have to apply the glue in the right quantities. Too much glue and the crack will be noticeable; too little glue and the bond may not hold. In this context, non-Torah people are not lucky enough to realize that Jewish law in all its details concerning marital intimacy insures that the right amount of glue will be applied; it is a program of discipline designed to perfect the spiritual and replenish the physical.[39]

I once spoke with a non-Jewish marriage counselor who admitted that fact to me. He said that the *halachic* guidelines were the healthiest way he had ever encountered for a couple to live. The obligation to withdraw from an opportunity for physical enjoyment, when the Torah prescribes such withdrawal, kindles the flame which unites the half-souls.

If you notice, this is the reverse of the attitude prevalent in the non-Torah world. To be more specific, many secular people today are not afraid to admit that, as they view it, the goal of marriage is the pleasure of physical intimacy. Even if they don't admit it publicly many still think it.

Yes, children are nice, but since, as they say, the real object is to enjoy life, and there is no higher type of enjoyment they can imagine, they view this pleasure as an end in itself — the highest *end*. Some may limit themselves because there is a question of how much they can get away with. However, deep down, according to a secular viewpoint, there is no real reason to refrain from any enjoyment which may come one's way.

The Torah also says to enjoy life, but the enjoyment is a *means* to the end. The "end" in terms of marriage, according to the Torah, is to reunite the two half-souls, and make them one again. That can only occur through giving to each other totally unselfishly. If personal satisfaction comes at the expense of the needs of one's spouse or of the needs of one's soul, it is unjustified and ultimately destructive. True, life is for enjoying, but with limits; the limits create real, everlasting enjoyment — they even enrich the physical pleasure.

On the other hand, people who pursue physical pleasure as an end not only never attain it, but get no rest in their futile pursuit. Physical pleasures evaporate like cold air in the winter; they seem to have substance, but quickly disappear before their eyes. All they leave behind is the damage they caused and an insatiable appetite for more, an appetite which does not go away easily.

Torah is the food of the soul. Feed your soul Torah — live by its guidelines — and you will quell the demands of the body. Every time you give up a little of yourself, a little of your body's self, you gain. You become one with your soul-partner.

The Oneness of the Cherubim

MOSHE: But even using your analogy of the broken vase, how can you say that the original crack will not be seen?

RABBI: Museums are filled with proof that it is possible. As I said, it all depends on a clean surface, and applying the right quantities of glue — along with the diligence and patience to do it. If done properly, not only will the original crack be invisible, but the area of the bond will be stronger than before. If that is true for physical objects, it is even more so for the soul.

A couple has to become one just as the *cherubim* were one.[40] The *cherubim* were the two angelic figures — one male and one female — on top of the ark which contained the tablets incscribed with the ten commandments. The *cherubim* and the cover of the ark were actually hammered out from a single piece of gold; it was forbidden to solder any part of them. So, too, a couple is originally one soul; they are not two entities melted and molded together. They can become one just as the *cherubim* were one.

MOSHE: Doesn't it say that *Hashem's* voice emanated from a point between the two *cherubim*?[41]

RABBI: Yes. They were the connecting point between heaven and earth, the conduit for spirituality in this physical world. And so, too, when a couple attains true oneness the *Shechinah,* the Divine Presence, comes down into this world and dwells among them just as it did between the *cherubim.*

Furthermore, when the *Kohen Gadol* (the High Priest), once a year on Yom Kippur, entered the inner chamber of the Temple where the *cherubim* were situated, a miracle happened. If the love between *Hashem* and His people Israel was strong, the figures would be embracing each other; if not, they would be turned away from one another. So, too, when the love between a man and a woman is strong, and is the kind of love that produces spiritual reunion and oneness, then they and their household are worthy of having the Divine Presence manifest Itself in their lives like It manifested Itself in the Temple. And that level of unity is the meaning of "to become one."

Keeping the Glue Strong

MOSHE: Rabbi, you make a lot of sense. Why then is it so easy to run into problems in a marriage?

RABBI: In the Torah world, problems begin when we let ourselves be influenced by the outside world. Marriages where the couple is true to the Torah ideal are far happier and more fulfilling than anything Hollywood or Madison Avenue can come up with.

The motif of the secular world is, "If you've got it, flaunt it." Exposure is the ideal. Even insulated communities cannot remain totally unaffected by this widespread attitude. Therefore, it is no wonder that an unprecedented number of marriages even in our communities dissolve or exist under tremendous strain. The dominant society seduces us into releasing the grip on our desires.

Torah does not tell you to repress your desires; it tells you to reserve it for your spouse. There is a reason that *Hashem* gave you a desire — keep it, hold onto it — but it was given to you in order to save it for your spouse. If you turn that desire toward others, you thin out the glue that was intended to solidify the bond between husband and wife. Thin glue will make a shaky bond.

It takes enormous willpower and cunning to avoid situations and external stimuli which tap into the pool of your desires. And when you do give yourself up to them — through our eyes, ears, imagination, bodies, etc. — you naturally feel less satisfied with your spouse, and have less desire. Your spouse, in turn, senses your weakened desire and reduces his or her own desires, starting a cycle which perpetuates itself to the point where two good people meant for each other do not want to stay together any longer.

For many people, this is where the battle is won or lost. And if their marriage breaks up because they could not control their imaginations, their second marriage will not be successful either. The same temptations will haunt them then also. The only solution is to guard your eyes and heart now.

CHAPTER 4

WOMAN

The "Good" of Man

SHAINA: Rabbi, I couldn't agree more about how easy it is to be influenced by the outside world without even knowing it. I have to admit that sometimes I find myself thinking how much the world clashes with some of the things our rabbis and teachers taught us in school. To get to the point, sometimes I struggle with the role the Torah has for women.

RABBI: Unfortunately that it is not unusual.

SHAINA: I wonder if my insecurity about the woman's role causes some of our problems.

RABBI: That is a possibility.

SHAINA: Then perhaps you can help me in this regard.

RABBI: The best way to feel good about the Torah's outlook on anything is to understand it better; and to realize the true motivations behind the non-Torah attitude.

Let me give you one example. Once, a *baales teshuva,* a woman who became Torah-observant — who also happened to be a successful career woman — told me something shocking. She said that in the secular world a woman is ready for marriage when she can afford a divorce.

I had to check if I heard correctly. However, I quickly realized that she had really hit upon something. The unspoken, underlying motivation behind the emphasis on independence and women's careers today, all too often, is that it is a preparation for the eventuality of a divorce; she does not want to be dependent on the husband. Preparing for this eventuality, however, makes divorce more of a probability, if not an inevitability.

A woman is endowed with an extra need to be dependent on a man, as it says, "And your desire will be for your husband."[42] No one can avoid being dependent on something, and a woman even more so because of this curse. Letting go of her other dependencies in order to become dependent on her husband is crucial for building up the maximum desire between the couple.

On the other hand, nowadays, many elements in society teach women to distrust men, and maybe given the history of men in the non-Jewish, non-Torah civilization they have some justification for that stance. However, a Jew has to live up to his and her own standards, not worrying what others think. Jewish men imbued with Torah are not wife-beaters. Jewish women who epitomize modesty and look up to their husbands are in no way devalued or regarded as second-class people. On the contrary, the secularists talk about equality, but do they realize that their emphasis on equality devalues women in comparison to the Torah's opinion of woman, which teaches that woman is not the equal of man, but the better half.

SHAINA: Hmm. That's interesting. Please explain.

RABBI: It's not my idea. It is stated clearly in the Torah. The Hebrew word for "bone" (*etzem*) — popularly translated as "rib" — means "essence." When *Hashem* took the rib from Adam to create a woman, He took the best part, the *etzem*, the "essence." Later, when she is shown to Adam, he remarks that she is "essence of my essence." The woman is the essence of their Divine soul. She is literally the "good" of man.

SHAINA: What do you mean she is the "good" of man?

RABBI: Before the creation of Chava, the Torah says of Adam, "It is not good (*lo tov*) being man alone." Man, without the ability to give, is labeled "not good." He only becomes "good" (*tov*) when he marries the

women. The woman removes his label of "not good"
and returns him to the category of "good" because she
is the "good," she is the *tov*.

The Diamond of the Couple

SHAINA: I'm still not perfectly clear about what you
mean when you say that the woman is the "good", the
tov of man?

RABBI: If I could compare it, it is like a diamond and a
ring. A diamond ring is valued according to the worth
of the diamond; the ring is only there to house the
diamond. For instance, suppose the diamond becomes
separated from the ring. Which part is missing
something?

SHAINA: The ring?

RABBI: Yes. It is virtually worthless now. The diamond,
however, did not lose any value; it is not missing
anything. It can be placed in a pin, an earring, etc. It
is the diamond which fills the ring and gives it worth.

Now, think for a second: In comparing a husband
and wife, who would you expect to be the diamond,
and who the ring?

SHAINA: I'm not sure.

RABBI: The ring is the husband, and the diamond is the
wife. She is the "good" of the couple. Without her, he
is like a ring without the diamond; he only attains
value — he only leaves his state of being "not good"

— when the diamond is placed in the prongs. Did you ever see a person wearing four prongs with no diamond in the middle? That is a man until he is married.

This, by the way, illustrates why according to *halacha* only the mother determines the status of the children. As the diamond, only she determines the essence of the soul. Conversely, if a Jewish man marries a non-Jewish woman he produces non-Jewish children. That is because it is only the diamond, the essence, which produces and determines the essence of the offspring.

Another extension of this analogy is the permissibility in ancient times of one man to marry more than one woman. A ring can be studded with several diamonds. However, did you ever see one diamond with several rings?

Furthermore, only a man, in the strict *halachic* sense, has the commandment to get married. A woman does not. We can understand it perfectly now. A man without his essence, like a ring without its diamond, has nothing — no joy, blessing, good or Torah. The woman is not commanded by strict Jewish law to be married because the diamond has value even without the ring.

Of course, what happens if the diamond is loose and is not kept in a vault? Or if it is in the ring but loosely fitted? Both the ring and the diamond are destined for tragedy. The ring will lose its value, and the diamond, if "she" does not let herself settle into the ring, may fall out. Although she still retains her value she may be lost in the street and eventually stepped on, stolen, or misused.

Aishes chail ateres baalah, "A woman of valor is the crown of her husband."[43] The woman is not inferior; she is the diamond of the couple.

Shelo Osani Ishah

SHAINA: Why then does a man say, *shelo osani ishah*, blessing *Hashem* every morning "for not making [me] a woman"?

RABBI: That blessing has nothing to do with the stature of a person; in fact, the focus of the blessing is not the person at all. We are thanking *Hashem* for the *mitzvos* He gave us.

SHAINA: How is that?

RABBI: The blessing *shelo osani ishah* is the third blessing in an increasing progression of thanks for being given so many commandments by *Hashem*. Thus, we first thank Him that we do not have a mere seven commandments like the non-Jew, and then we thank Him for not having the reduced number of commandments that the servant has. Jewish men are commanded all 613 *mitzvos* — and that is something to truly thank *Hashem* for.

The proof that the blessings are reflective of our

thanks for receiving an abundance of *mitzvos* and not of the misconception that the third blessing reflects the so-called lower status of women is the law, according to some opinions, that if the man skips either one or both of the prior two blessings — regarding non-Jews and servants — he does not repeat them. The reason is because the third blessing, *shelo osani ishah*, includes the first two; he cannot say these three blessings in any order he wishes because the order is reflective of a progression concerning the number of *mitzvos*.

MOSHE: Even so, the problem still remains, because women are not commanded in *mitzvos asay shehazman grama*, positive commandments requiring an action to be performed at some specific time. Thus, they have fewer *mitzvos* than men.

RABBI: The fact that man has more commandments is not reflective of higher status. On the contrary, the woman is more naturally on the higher level, and that is why only she thanks *Hashem* for creating her *k'rtzono,* "according to His will." The Jewish man needs all the *mitzvos* to help him get back to the point where he is in line with *Hashem*'s will and desire. The woman, as the diamond of the couple, is freed from certain positive commandments which the man needs to make himself diamond-like.

SHAINA: But, according to your reasoning, wouldn't non-Jews and servants be on an even higher level because they need even fewer commandments?

RABBI: No. A *Yisroel oved Hashem*, as I explained earlier, performs *Hashem*'s will in a way nothing else in creation can. Within *Yisroel oved Hashem* the male and female have different paths through which to perform *Hashem*'s will and reach completion. That, and that alone, is what is reflected in the different blessings which a Jewish man and a Jewish woman say.

Women and Groupings

SHAINA: I have another question, then. If women are not regarded as less than men, why can't they be accepted as witnesses in a Jewish court of law?

RABBI: Let me ask you this: If you were marrying off your child and were given the choice of having Moses and Aaron as witnesses to the ceremony, would you take them?

SHAINA: Of course.

RABBI: Then your child would not be married because, being brothers, they are disqualified as witnesses in a Jewish court of law.[44] Now, no one was more trustworthy than Moses and Aaron, yet you see clearly from this that the determination of the status of Jewish witnesses is not dependent upon considerations of trustworthiness.[45]

SHAINA: Then what does determine it?

RABBI: The entire determination is called a *chok*, a statute whose reasons go beyond the ability of human reason to comprehend. The truth is that for simple testimony needed to establish a fact — is this item *kosher* or not, who made it, where was it made, etc. — one witness is accepted. And wherever one person is accepted, a woman is similarly accepted.

MOSHE: Doesn't the Torah require two witnesses?

RABBI: Only in cases where the Torah says "Upon two witnesses the matter is established"[46] — like marriage and money matters — does this *chok,* this special rule requiring two witnesses, apply. In cases not referred to by that verse, one witness can establish a fact, and that one witness can be a woman.

SHAINA: Even with that explanation, though, there still must be a reason why *Hashem* chose to exclude women as witnesses in those cases rather than include them.

RABBI: *Hashem's* reason for giving us a *chok* is beyond us. However, the general principle is as I have been trying to explain to you all along, namely, that women are the diamond of the couple, the essence, and are therefore basically complete even alone. Men, on the other hand, are fragments by themselves. Therefore, regarding testimony requiring at least two witnesses, only men are counted because only men, as incomplete entities, can be combined to form a whole testimonial group. A woman, who is a complete unit by herself, is not combined and made into one larger whole. *Hashem* created her whole by herself, *k'rtzono* (according to His will).

Similarly, in any area of Jewish life where a count is required — like testimonial groups, a minyan for prayer, etc. — women are not included because they are already complete. Only fragments of a whole have this obligation and ability to be joined at specific times to form a single group.

Inner Holiness

SHAINA: Okay. Now, what about those who say that the woman's role in the home is secondary to the man's role?

RABBI: Anyone who is not afraid to admit it can clearly see that the home is where everything starts. It is by no means a secondary assignment to be charged with the responsibility to build, nurture and protect it.

Consider this: Every nation has a Minister of the Exterior and a Minister of the Interior. The Minister of the Exterior is charged with projecting the proper image of the nation to the international community. The Minister of the Interior is the maker and molder of that image. If there is no national character, then the Minister of the Exterior is a fraud.

Similarly, *Hashem* chose the Jewish nation to represent Him in this world: "You shall be a kingdom of *Kohanim* (priestly class) and a holy nation."[47] The verse says in effect that every Jewish male is charged with the mission of the *kohen* class — to be representatives of the holiness of the Jewish nation. In this sense, then, men, like the *Kohanim,* are the Ministers of the Exterior. The Jewish woman, on the other hand, is the Minister of the Interior. She is molder of the inner character of the "holy nation" (*goy kadosh*). Without her there is no holiness for the "kingdom of *Kohanim*" to represent.

Man, as Minister of the Exterior, is in charge of sanctifying *Hashem*'s name in the outside world. Woman, as Minister of the Interior, is in charge of building the home, where the essential character and strength of the *goy kadosh* will be nurtured. Of course, just as in national entities these two departments need to confer with, exchange information, and advise each other, so, too, the husband and wife. At times they may even be called upon to temporarily perform the other's job. However, each has a primary assignment.

It is like a pilot and navigator: Even though the final decision is the pilot's, the navigator can have great influence on that decision. So, too, the man is the pilot when it comes to going out in the world and making a mark, and the woman is the navigator. Conversely, the woman is pilot when it comes to raising children and setting the tone of the house, while the man is the navigator.

This is why it is so important that the woman's exposure to outside elements be limited. To perform her job, she has to work from within herself to thereby insure that the internal character remains secure.

SHAINA: Rabbi, what would you say to a modern woman who claims that the things you are saying are only a rationale to keep women locked up in the home?

RABBI: I'm not talking about staying locked up in a house. In today's times, inside versus outside is not defined simply by physical location. With television, videos, magazines and newspapers a person can bring all the garbage from the outside world to the inside.

Inside means secluded from the world. A woman who goes out into the world does not have to lose her orientation of *tzniyus* — her inner, hidden holiness. She can be outside and yet fortify her mind and heart so that she is unaffected. It is possible for a career woman to serve as an example of inner Jewish beauty, while it is also possible for a secluded housewife to allow Times Square to be brought into her house.

SHAINA: Isn't *tzniyus* modesty?

RABBI: Yes.

SHAINA: But you just referred to it as inner holiness.

RABBI: A woman's holiness is her modesty, as it says, "The entire glory of the king's daughter is on the inside."[48] Her devotion to inner values earns her true recognition and honor.

The Tablets and the Menorah

SHAINA: Can you elaborate on this idea?

RABBI: Yes. The Jewish home is a miniature *Bais Hamikdash*, a miniature Temple. The Temple housed four objects, three of which were in the *kodesh,* or outer chamber, and one in the *kodesh hakadoshim* — the Holy of Holies — the inner chamber entered only once a year by the *Kohen Gadol* on Yom Kippur. The three objects in the outer chamber were the *shulchan* (table), the incense altar, and the *menorah.* They represent the three pillars upon which the world stands.[49]

The *shulchan*-table represents charity (*gemilus chasadim*), the incense altar symbolizes the Divine service (*avodah*), and the *menorah* stands for Torah. In the inner chamber the fourth object, the ark of the covenant, rested; it also represents Torah but in a different form than the *menorah.*

SHAINA: How is that?

RABBI: The *menorah* represents the man's Torah, because the *menorah* gives off light to the outside. The man has to go out to learn in *yeshiva* and spread his Torah outside the home, just as a lamp spreads its light.

The ark represents the woman's Torah. Itself hidden in the innermost chamber of the Holy Temple, the stones in the ark were engraved with the writing of *Hashem.* They stand for, and in fact are, the essence of Torah. They are the core from which all else radiates.

A man, like the *menorah* spreading its light in the darkness, can only reveal the essence. A woman, like the tablets, *is* the essence. A man's Torah, explaining and spreading to the outside, is the external aspect of Torah; a woman, being a monument of Torah values, is the internal aspect of Torah.

It is interesting to note that the ark was never desecrated and taken from the Jews when the Temple was destroyed. It had been buried and hidden before the destruction of the First Temple. However, the *menorah,* as well as many other vessels, were taken into exile. The deeper idea behind this is that exile has affected and deteriorated the man's Torah while the woman's Torah has remained untouched, and is in fact indestructible. Allow me to explain.

It is an undisputed fact that as the generations have gone by, the level of Torah scholarship has declined. The rabbis of the *Talmud* were not empowered to overrule the rabbis of the *Mishna.* The early *Talmudic* commentators could not dispute a decision rendered by the rabbis of the *Talmud.* The later commentators are not equal to the early ones, and so on. This is the present deteriorated condition of man's Torah.

The woman's Torah, however, is not so. Hers is the internal Torah; she delivers the holy souls down into this world thereby building from the inside the *goy kadosh,* the holy nation. That is her Torah. Therefore, when even the simplest Jewish woman with her simple faith follows the *halacha* regarding family purity, she fulfills her task no less than any of the great Jewish women throughout history.

I often use this idea to explain why biographies of Torah giants are only of men. The wife of the Vilna Gaon, for instance, was every bit as great as her illustrious husband, however, the story of her life is not published and told. The reason, I feel, is because the purpose of a biography is to document people and events the likes of which we will never see again. No man in our time can even hope to approach the Torah scholarship of the Vilna Gaon, and therefore we need a biography of him.

The role of the woman, though, has not deteriorated. The soul which a Jewish woman brings down into the world today is potentially just as pure as a Jewish soul which came down 200 or 2,000 years ago. Only the garment of the soul — its nature and ability to function in this world — which is dependent on the Torah which the father transmits,[50] has become progressively weaker.

Therefore, a biography of the wife of the Vilna Gaon, written to commemorate a level of greatness which was lost, is not necessary, because women have never lost their greatness. They can fulfill their essential role today no less than Sarah, Rivka, Rachel and Leah. Exile has affected the external Torah, the Torah of the man; it has not touched the internal Torah, the Torah of the woman.

That is why it is so important for each individual Jewish woman not to desire to imitate the man's Torah. She is the carrier of the spark that *Hashem* gave as an unconditional gift to the seed of Abraham, Isaac, and Jacob. She is — and must nurture and protect — that pure inner holiness.

In a similar sense, what does America do with its most important secrets? They are buried in a safe somewhere in the Pentagon in Washington. Likewise, the woman, who is the essence of the holy nation, must stay within herself and not simply expose her secrets to the outside.

Picture a beautiful orchard which is completely burned up by fire, and all that remains is one little seed. As long as the owner takes that seed and puts it in a vault, there is hope the orchard can be replanted anew.

The ark hidden away, like the Torah of the Jewish woman, is that hope. Her decision to be modest in the face of a world which seeks to seduce her into exposing and thereby demeaning her true inner beauty is like putting the seed — the essence and secret — of the Jewish people in a vault. That is why the Sages says that in the merit of righteous women we were redeemed from Egypt,[51] and in their merit the future redemption will take place. She is our link to the past and our hope for the future.

Kiddush Hashem

SHAINA: The truth is, rabbi, that I always knew the Torah valued women highly —

RABBI: How do you know?

SHAINA: How do *I* know?

RABBI: Yes, how do you know?

SHAINA: Well, for instance, in the discussion between Abraham and Sarah, *Hashem* told Abraham to listen to whatever Sarah said because she had greater prophetic powers. And also when Yitzchak wanted to give his blessing to Esav, it was his wife who saw through Esav's false mask of reverence and realized that Jacob was the true heir to these blessings.

RABBI: Very good. It is vital to keep that in mind and not to pay attention to people and outside influences who really have no connection to Torah.

SHAINA: I do . . . or at least I try to. What I mean is that sometimes it is hard to translate that into reality.

RABBI: That is not only your problem; it is everyone's problem, both men and women. Men have that problem to a greater extent in their careers, and women in the home. Faced with the conflict between reality and idealism many people buckle under and abandon their ideals. However, the battle is won only when we hold onto and strengthen our ideals, and thereby make reality a little sweeter. Doing so makes things better for our children, our spouses, and ultimately ourselves.

SHAINA: How does one sweeten reality with Torah ideals?

RABBI: Learn. Understand. Fill your mind with thoughts that give meaning to your actions. Let me delve into this subject for a few moments so you will have something to keep in mind which sweetens your ability to be a fulfilled Jew and, especially, to be a fulfilled Jewish woman.

SHAINA: Go ahead.

RABBI: What is the magic word for a Jewish person?

SHAINA: What do you mean by "magic word"?

RABBI: In business, for example, the magic word is money. Businesses have many divisions: the buying division, the selling division, the marketing division, the accounting division, etc. What does the chief executive always have to keep in mind whenever he makes a decision regarding any component of his business?

MOSHE: He has to ask: How will this make money?

RABBI: Yes. When he buys, he tries to buy cheap. When he sells, he tries to sell expensive. Even a business which truly serves the public can only continue to do so as long as it makes money. If the decision-maker forgets this magic word the service will come to a halt. Therefore, all decisions, one way or another, must be weighed against the measurement of how much money will be earned.

Now, what is the magic word for a Jewish person, a word that cuts across all divisions, including man's role, woman's role, private behavior, public behavior, etc.?

SHAINA: I don't know?

RABBI: The answer is *kiddush Hashem*, to sanctify G-d's name.

SHAINA: Please explain.

RABBI: As I told you earlier, *Hashem* created the world, but the world is really Him. However, *Hashem* can never be completely absent. In some way He always remains hidden in His world. And that is why the Hebrew word for world is *olam*, which also means "hidden."

Man is a partner with *Hashem* in that he has the chore of refining the world, to "fill the earth and conquer it."[52] How does he conquer and refine the world? Through "filling" the spiritual void created by *Hashem*'s hiddenness. Allowing *Hashem* to remain hidden is called *chillul Hashem*. *Chillul*, explains the Zohar, is related to the word *chalal*, meaning void or emptiness. Any place in the world where G-dliness is not seen — that is *chillul Hashem*.

The opposite of *chillul Hashem* is *kiddush Hashem*. Any place where man discovers *Hashem* — where man conducts his life according to *Hashem*'s will — that is *kiddush Hashem*. Through *kiddush Hashem*, revealing

G-d, man "fills the world," he fills in the *chalal*, the void, which otherwise is this world. That is the way man becomes a partner with *Hashem* in creation.

The *kaddish* prayer we recite several times a day — *Amen, yehay shmai raba m'vorach l'olam ulolmay olmoyah*, "Amen, may His great name be blessed forever and ever" — is the great declaration, the battle cry, of the Jew. It is the one reverberating thought we must take with us wherever we go, because every area or experience in our lives which may look purely physical or empty of G-dliness can be sanctified. The *kaddish* reminds us that *kiddush Hashem* is the magic word cutting across all components of our life.

Therefore, *kiddush Hashem* is the idea of discovering *Hashem*, of affirming His existence. Now, what is the highest type of *kiddush Hashem* you can imagine?

MOSHE: Sacrificing one's life for *Hashem*'s sake?

RABBI: That is true, but short of giving up your life, what is one of the great ways of affirming *Hashem*'s existence in this life?

SHAINA: Doing *mitzvos*?

RABBI: I'm looking for something which includes the *mitzvos;* a way in which the *mitzvos* can be performed which itself is a *kiddush Hashem*?

SHAINA: I give up.

MOSHE: So do I.

RABBI: Any righteous act performed when nobody else is looking, the Rambam writes,[53] is one of the great forms of *kiddush Hashem.*

SHAINA: What makes a private act so great?

RABBI: Because people are naturally disposed to doing
things based on what others will think of them. Secular
politics are filled with such people. They seem
dedicated to the pursuit of higher ideals, however,
when you look into the private lives of many of them,
you find out how morally bankrupt they were or are.
They were idealistic because they received public
recognition for being so. True Torah leaders are just
the opposite. While in no way lacking in ideals, the
more you look into their private lives, the more you
find their real greatness.

Actions performed in private are the barometer of
greatness because they prove that the person had
Hashem in mind, and only *Hashem* in mind; they
affirm *Hashem*'s existence. A man, for instance, can
perform a great *kiddush Hashem* when he is walking
down the street, and he comes upon a newsstand
displaying unbecoming images. Although no one else
would know one way or the other, he averts his eyes.
That affirms his recognition that *Hashem* is operating
in his life; that is a *kiddush Hashem.*

MOSHE: Even though no one knows about it? I thought
kiddush Hashem meant public sanctification of
Hashem?

RABBI: That misconception is what the Rambam comes
to dispel: The essential idea behind sanctifying *Hashem*

is performing His will under even the most difficult circumstances. Private acts are in some ways the most difficult of circumstances. One who carries out *Hashem*'s will when no one is looking fills the spiritual void of this world. That is *kiddush Hashem* in the ultimate sense, filling the *chalal* by living as if *Hashem* is in our lives especially where He seems to be most absent or hidden.

The Woman's Unique Kiddush Hashem

Now, you should know that a woman in her role is entrusted with a *mitzvah* which produces *kiddush Hashem* more than anything a man does.

SHAINA: What *mitzvah* is that?

RABBI: *Taharas haMishpacha*, family purity laws. Let me illustrate to you the enormity of what I am saying.

Jewish law states that one is not allowed to lend money to a friend without witnesses if he is not willing to forgive him should the friend deny that he was given the loan. If I lent you $100 dollars without witnesses, since you could easily deny it, it is considered as if I am tempting you to deny it. And if you do deny it, it was I who aided you to become a thief. That is helping another to come to sin, and I am forbidden to do so.

This law is based on a keen insight into human nature: temptation can affect anyone. Therefore, don't tempt temptation.

Now, what is the greatest investment that *Hashem* has in this world? His *goy kadosh*, His holy nation. The holy nation is built through family purity laws which insure and protect the holiness of the souls brought down into this world. And whom did *Hashem* trust with this great investment? The woman; and no one woman in particular, but every Jewish woman.

Hashem tells her, "I am putting My trust in you. You don't even need witnesses. The preparations necessary for immersing in the *mikveh* — which establishes the very holiness of My nation — is entirely in your hands."

Think about it. A man is not trusted to lend $50 without witnesses even to a friend because of the temptation to deny it; and if he does so he transgresses Jewish law. Yet *Hashem* entrusts the entire physical and emotional needs of a human being into the hands of a woman.

I know of a young couple who became Torah-observant after they had been married. They took up all the Torah laws including *taharas haMishpacha* with genuine love. Immediately, unavoidable complications arose in the woman's preparations, keeping the couple apart. A few weeks passed. Then a few months. After five months, the couple was under tremendous strain. Finally, when it looked like the matter would be resolved, a question concerning her preparations came

up — she saw a suspicious spot — and she
approached the *Rav*. He told her that unfortunately
they had to wait even longer.

Now, this woman could have easily denied it; she
didn't have to go to the *Rav*. Her marriage was under
strain and if she imagined that she didn't see the
suspicious spot no one would have known. Yet, she
didn't deny it. That sacrifice on her part was
superhuman because the only other one who would
have known was *Hashem*. She protected His interests.
She assured the holiness of the souls which she is
responsible for delivering into this world. That act in
private was a great *kiddush Hashem*.

Moshe, I see something is bothering you.

MOSHE: No. Let's go on.

RABBI: Are you sure? I'll be more than happy to answer
your questions.

MOSHE: It's not worth it.

RABBI: Whatever you say. Now —

MOSHE: For five months they were separated?

RABBI: I thought something was bothering you.

MOSHE: What did *Hashem* want from the poor couple?

RABBI: First, as you know, that type of situation is very,
very rare.

MOSHE: True.

RABBI: Second, *Hashem* knows what a person or couple
is really capable of. He can look in their hearts and
know how much is too much. When He gives tests like

the one this couple had to undergo His intention is to bring latent greatness to the surface. *Hashem* tested Abraham with the same intentions: not for His sake, and not even for Abraham's sake, but in order to show the world Abraham's previously hidden greatness.

Hashem knows the truth; He tests people to show them and others who they are. He saw the deep, deep devotion that this *baal teshuva* couple had, and gave them this test in order to bring out their beauty. When *Hashem* sends a difficult test, He knows the person has the ability to overcome it and make an even greater *kiddush Hashem*.

The greater the sacrifice, the greater the sanctification. King Solomon wrote: *Ner Hashem nishmas adam*, "A lamp of *Hashem* is the soul of man."[54] The Zohar explains that the wick corresponds to the body, the flame is the soul, and the oil the *mitzvos* or deeds that a person performs.

Now, the quality of a lamp's light is first dependent on the purity of the oil. The more the olive is beaten and crushed the finer the oil it produces. So, too, regarding *mitzvos*. The greater the difficulty in performing them, the purer the oil and the brighter the spiritual light. Furthermore, just as the more the wick burns and nullifies itself, the more it sheds light, so, too, the more the body, as a metaphor to the wick, gives up of itself, the more spiritual light it sheds.

Imagine how much light this *baal teshuva* couple

shed by remaining apart based solely on their new-found conviction in Torah. Add to that the particular brilliance of the wife's *kiddush Hashem* by acting trustworthily. She could have cheated so easily, yet by overcoming herself she made the greatest proclamation of *Hashem*'s dominion in this world.

Entering the Holy of Holies

Now, don't think that only a woman in this type of situation can perform such a *kiddush Hashem*. This woman had particularly difficult challenges making her act even greater, however, any Jewish woman who prepares herself through *taharas haMishpacha* before going to the *mikveh* performs this unique type of *kiddush Hashem*.

SHAINA: Is it really more unique than any other type of private *kiddush Hashem*?

RABBI: Yes, *Divrei HaYamim*, the Book of Chronicles, calls the *kodesh hakadoshim*, the Holy of Holies, which is the inner chamber of the holy Temple, the *cheder hamitos*, literally "the bedroom."[55] This statement draws a parallel between the actions of a wife and the *Kohen Gadol*. The *Kohen Gadol* was the holiest Jew. For seven days, he purified himself and meditated in preparation for performing the most important act on the most important day of the year — entering the Holy of Holies on Yom Kippur.

Today, it is virtually impossible to comprehend the enormity of this mission, but the entire nation's — the entire world's — sanctity and well-being rested on the performance of the *Kohen Gadol* when he entered the Holy of Holies. More difficult for the modern mind to comprehend is that it was a completely private act; no one would know if he actually performed the required ceremonies, and just as significantly, no one would see if he had the purity of thought which was required to fulfill his awesome responsibility — no one, that is, except *Hashem*. Yet, the nation's holiness rested on the private thoughts and acts of this one individual.

Similarly, every married Jewish woman undertakes the same process not once a year and not only when the Temple stood, but regularly, even nowadays. Just as the *Kohen Gadol* prepared seven days before entering the *cheder hamitos,* she also goes through a seven day preparation period, in anticipation of her visit to the *mikveh.* Furthermore, just as the nation's holiness rested on the private actions of the *Kohen Gadol*, so, too, the nation's present state of holiness is dependent on her private actions. In fact, whenever she goes through this process, it is as if *Hashem* takes her on as a partner in bearing witness to the holiness of the Jewish people. And this is her *chok,* her unique way of fulfilling the verse, "Through two witnesses will the matter be established."[56]

The Cleansing Waters

Moshe, I hope you appreciate this. Our connection to the holiness of the *Kohen Gadol* on Yom Kippur is through our wives. Each time she undergoes this process, intimacy between husband and wife becomes not only a glue for their relationship but a means of "filling the earth" with *kiddush Hashem*, and reuniting the physical with the spiritual.

MOSHE: What do you mean "reuniting the physical with the spiritual"?

RABBI: This is the idea of *mikveh.* The Torah begins, "In the beginning *Hashem* created the heaven and earth." Heaven — the spiritual — and earth — the physical — were originally one and undivided. "And the earth was desolate, void, and dark" the Torah continues. This means that *Hashem*, so to speak, emptied out the physical world of spirituality; as we said, He hid Himself. Later, *Hashem* commands mankind to "fill the earth," to fill this emptied out area, as I explained to you earlier.[57]

Now, the physical and spiritual are so different. How can one fill the other? The answer is because *Hashem* created a medium, something which bridges the gap between these two opposites. Water.

Rain water, which falls down to the earth, is still attached to the heavenly elements. Pure, unpolluted water never drawn by man or placed in a container of any type is the one thing in this world which mirrors the spiritual. Thus, the Torah says, "And the spirit of *Hashem* hovered above the water."

Therefore, if a person became submerged in the physicality of this earth, water is the element by which he or she can reconnect to the spiritual realm. Submerging in the waters of a *mikveh* is like dipping oneself temporarily in heaven. People reattach themselves to their spiritual root, the place where their souls originated. This cleanses them of any defilement they may have suffered due to immersion in the physical.

The concept of *mikveh,* then, is to link heaven and earth, to allow heaven a foothold down here on this earth. That is the purpose of the Temple, epitomized by the service of the *Kohen Gadol* on Yom Kippur. And the process of purification which the *Kohen Gadol* went through to link heaven to earth is the model for the process which Jewish law requires a woman to undergo before she is ready to bring a pure, unpolluted heavenly soul into this physical world.[58]

CHAPTER 5

COMMON PROBLEMS — PRACTICAL STRATEGIES

MOSHE: Rabbi, please excuse me one moment. I know we are not finished, but I have to make an important call.

SHAINA: Now?

MOSHE: I didn't know the session would last so long.

SHAINA: But, do you have to go now?

MOSHE: Yes. It's important.

SHAINA: Moshe, there is always something more important. What about our relationship? Isn't that important?

MOSHE: This will be quick . . . I think.

SHAINA: It never is.

MOSHE: But if I don't make calls like this we won't have

an income.

SHAINA: Can't you hold off on one call? Rabbi, I'm glad this came up because this is one of the things we always quarrel about. It is one of the things that really bothers me about Moshe.

MOSHE: If you want to get into the things that bother me we can get into that, too.

RABBI: Listen, getting angry at each other now will not get us anywhere. Obviously there is a problem here, otherwise you would not have come to me. It is time to turn our focus to some of your specific problems, and try to alleviate the immediate tension so you can begin to work on the things we have discussed. In your opinion, what is the real sore spot in this marriage?

SHAINA: I would say it is that Moshe puts other things in ahead of our marriage.

RABBI: Let's try to do this without accusing each other. See if you can come up with something that both of you agree is disappointing about your marriage, and let's try to begin to work on it.

MOSHE: I would say that the first real problem we have to work out is the daily conflicts.

SHAINA: I agree with that. But, it's not just that we have conflicts, rabbi, it's the way we fight sometimes, the shouting and yelling.

MOSHE: Yes.

RABBI: With two individuals living in such close proximity to each other on a daily basis it is virtually impossible not to have different opinions. However, among other things, successful couples learn how to become negotiators.

SHAINA: What do you mean by that?

MOSHE: Yes. Can you explain further?

RABBI: A good negotiator is one who is quiet and listens. The one who always screams never hears anything. Too often husband and wife fight and scream rather than negotiate; everyone is broadcasting and no one is receiving. We are excited, we think we are right, and we think that since we are right, if we repeat it a little louder, then we will convince the other. It turns into a vicious cycle. Both parties are broadcasters, and the only ones receiving are the little children who grow up to be big broadcasters just like their parents.

SHAINA: What can we do about it, then?

RABBI: Become a good negotiator, a good listener. Suppose you're arguing over something — not just out of frustration or disgust — but you really think you are right. In that case, say to your spouse, "I'm sorry, I didn't understand that. Can you please repeat it?" If your spouse still insists he or she is right, ask him or her to repeat it again. Keep on doing this. By the third or fourth time your spouse will see for himself or herself and understand. That makes a good negotiator.

SHAINA: But now we both know the same trick.

RABBI: Try it anyway. The point is: negotiate. Sit down and talk, communicate. Do not broadcast. If your spouse is overly emotional, accept that, remain calm, and utilize your negotiating skills. It may not be easy, but the first step toward improving your relationship probably depends on it.

Laying the Foundation

MOSHE: Rabbi, obviously up to this point, our marriage to this point has been a failure in many ways. You have stressed to us several times about how much hard work it entails, but aren't there any easy solutions?

RABBI: Moshe, I visited Russia not too long ago, and something caught my attention. Virtually every wall of every building which had been put up since the Communist regime came to power was cracked or cracking. Furthermore, doors and windows very rarely closed snugly the way they were designed to. I asked one Russian about this.

He laughed.

"In Russia," he explained to me, "no one can make a living unless he steals. When the government puts up a building, however, it is difficult to take anything because they know exactly how many doors and windows are needed. If even one were missing it would be noticeable. So what can a Russian construction worker do? He steals from the foundation. A little less concrete is not noticeable — that is, it is not noticeable until a couple of years later when the walls begin to crack and the doors and windows stop fitting. In fact, that is why the earthquake in Armenia a few years ago was so devastating. Everyone stole from the foundation."

Cheating in the foundation, Moshe and Shaina, can never work in the long run. Not only will the structure itself begin to crack, but sometimes the building will crumble entirely. Too many couples try make-shift solutions; they read a book, discuss it with a confidante, even go to a marriage counselor, and implement different ideas in a patchwork fashion. They don't realize that the real work has to be done in the foundation.

MOSHE: What exactly do you mean by the foundation?

RABBI: Under the wedding canopy the couple is blessed that their marriage should be a *binyan adai ad*, "an everlasting structure." If you want to build a skyscraper one hundred stories high you cannot lay a foundation designed for a one or two-story structure. If indeed one's marriage is going to extend into the heavens, *adai ad,* then it is vital to lay the most solid of foundations. That foundation is a *shanah rishonah*, the first year of marriage.

The *shanah rishonah* is not just a good idea; it is a *mitzvah* in the Torah. The man is exempt from war, and, generally speaking, is freed from all public responsibilities so that he can give his wife his full attention in order to lay the foundation of his household. The better the couple get to know each other during the first year of marriage, the more solid their foundation. Then, they can start building the structure — adding on the bricks one by one, year after year — growing continuously in marriage.

MOSHE: What are you trying to tell us, rabbi? Our *shanah rishonah* passed and it is obvious that we did not lay the foundation properly. I think we both realize that it was a mistake. What can we do about it now, though?

RABBI: When an actual building begins to crack because the foundation is lacking, the first thing they do is brace the walls, and then pour new concrete into the foundation. Once the foundation is strengthened, repairs on the building itself can begin.

When a marriage starts getting cracks, focus has to be placed on refortifying the foundation — and not as much focus on the actual structure itself. The good news is that it is never too late for a couple to have a proper *shanah rishonah*. I know couples who first observed the *shanah rishonah* only after fifteen or twenty years of marriage. They sacrificed time in other areas of their lives in order to lay the foundation of their marriage. Admittedly, it is much harder if there are children and financial pressures, but determined people were able to overcome the difficulties, and completely renew their marriage.

SHAINA: Specifically, what does a *shanah rishonah* entail?

RABBI: Setting aside time for one another so that both of you can get to know each other. You have to really learn the other's likes and dislikes.

SHAINA: That makes sense.

RABBI: Before even that, however — and what I can best help you with right now — is you have to know the differences between men and women in general.

MOSHE: Doesn't the *Talmud* call women *Om bifnei atzmo.*[59]

RABBI: Yes.

SHAINA: What does that mean?

RABBI: It means that women are a "nation of their own." Let me explain: American culture shares much in common with British culture. Since, at the very least, both share a common language, an American in England will have to make only minor adjustments. If an American went to China or Japan, however, where real language and cultural barriers exist, he would need to make major adjustments in order to travel there.

One time I needed to travel to Thailand for ten days. As part of the requirement of travel I was given an orientation to teach me how to avoid insulting the people with simple mannerisms and actions which most foreigners and I take for granted as being acceptable. So, too, a newlywed couple have to learn about the ways and customs of this "independent nation" they are getting married to.

A man has absolutely no idea what a woman is. No man will experience bearing and giving birth to a child. Similarly, women have absolutely no idea what a man is. Neither really understands the deep needs of the other.

MOSHE: What do you mean? I may not know my wife and her particular habits, but I know my sister and my mother for instance.

RABBI: However, you did not marry them. Brother and sister don't have the attraction to each other that husband and wife have; therefore, they don't have the same needs. Similarly, you can't look at your wife and figure out her needs because you came to know your mother's needs. Your mother is your provider. Your wife is not your provider.

In fact, this is a common problem. Often, when men marry, they expect to be provided for like they were provided for by their mother. The man doesn't realize at first how a wife needs him because his mother never required of him the things a wife needs of a husband. When he marries, he takes it for granted that his wife will also not require of him things his mother did not require of him. That is a mistake of course.

Therefore, in order to understand her needs, a husband has to study his wife like he studies a *mesechta*, a volume of the *Talmud*. The man has to learn the *mesechta* called woman; the woman in turn has to study the *mesechta* called man. They are given one year each to study that *mesechta* and know it well. Of course, on top of the general differences between a man and a woman the couple comes into the marriage as two individuals who have individual quirks and needs, but for starters it is essential to realize the general differences.

Living With Your Spouse[60]

There are very many basic fundamental differences between the makeup of a man versus the makeup of a woman. Let me give you a few examples, and teach you a strategy for dealing successfully with these differences. First, let's examine some of the surface differences in their personalities.

Now, what I am about to tell you has its exceptions, however, I think most people agree that men tend to be more punctual than women.

SHAINA: That's true with us, I suppose.

MOSHE: Why would that be?

RABBI: I think the reason may be because a mother cannot afford to be dependent on a clock; she has to wake up in the middle of the night to feed the baby, and take care of its needs. This explains why the Torah doesn't obligate woman in positive commandments which have to be fulfilled at a specific time. A mother's job demands flexibility. A woman who insists on punctuality is going to become a very frustrated, anxious mother. Therefore, I would say that is why most women, by nature, tend to be less punctual than men.

Let me give you an example of this, and how understanding this fact can help you improve your relationship.

A husband will typically say to his wife, "We have to leave for the wedding tonight by seven o'clock." Seven o'clock rolls around and the husband is ready. He came home at ten to seven, changed his clothes, and was dressed in under ten minutes. The wife also began to get ready at ten to seven. By seven o'clock, though, she is nowhere near ready to leave. What happens next? The husband starts getting impatient.

"I told you seven o'clock," he says with obvious anger in his voice as the clock hits seven-thirty.

Now, if the husband understands that a woman, by nature, is less punctual than a man, he can avoid this problem and learn to compensate.

"Listen," he can tell her, "we have to leave for the wedding by twenty to seven." By five or ten after, she is ready to go.

MOSHE: But that is so obvious.

RABBI: Try it anyway. You will see that it always works.

The point I am trying to get across to you is that if the husband realizes that it is not only his wife who has trouble being on time — rather it is a problem that most women have — then he can deal with the situation and end up feeling less aggravated with her.

Let me give you another example of different tendencies in men and women. It is almost midnight towards the end of the week and the husband is about to get into bed. His wife is also up late, still in the kitchen baking and cooking for *Shabbos.* All of a sudden there is a piercing shriek from the kitchen.

His first thought is that a burglar has broken into the house. Dashing into the kitchen in his robe and slippers, he encounters his wife and sees a look of terror on her face.

"What's the matter?" he asks.

"A ca . . . a ca . . ."

"What?" he asks.

"A ca . . . a ca . . ."

"Say it already," he says, "What is it?"

"A ca . . . a cockroach! I saw a cockroach!"

The husband is completely still for a moment, trying to absorb what just transpired. What will most men do in that situation? Unfortunately, after he takes off his slipper and kills the cockroach, he may pick it up and dangle it in front of her before throwing it in the garbage. Then he really gives it to her.

"How in the world can you be so insensitive!? I was certain when you screamed just now that we were being burglarized by a band of armed robbers. How can you do that to me?"

Now, if he were to understand that most women are

scared of little creeping things, and that it has nothing to do with his wife in particular, then he would not get upset. His problem is that he does not realize that the nature of a woman is to be scared by these kinds of things.

Concerning the woman, I think that the majority of them would say, in their hearts at least, that their husbands are selfish. The fact is that women, by nature, are naturally selfless. The reason is probably because they bear children. *Hashem* therefore gave them a nature which wants to take care of and give to another. If a woman understood that when her husband demonstrates self-centeredness, it is not her husband alone, but most men who act that way, then she would be more at ease about it.

SHAINA: Are you justifying a man's selfishness?

RABBI: No. Not at all. He has to work to overcome his natural selfishness. What I am saying is that when he falls short of that goal, she should realize that many husbands are like that. It will help smooth the relationship so that they can both have enough space to improve themselves.

One other thing that women should be aware of is a man's greater need to have time alone. Women also need to be alone at times, but men, because of the way they are, tend to become more involved in their own world, be it business or learning, and have to be given the space to mull over that world.

SHAINA: Of course, he has to realize that she has a need to be let into that world; she wants some of his time, too.

RABBI: Yes, everyone's needs have to be taken into consideration. First, we have to realize that the other person does have needs different from ours; then we can begin to learn how to deal with them in a positive, healthy manner.

The Needs of Men and Women

RABBI: We have spoken about some of the differences between men and women. What would you say is a woman's most important need in a marriage?

MOSHE: I think she wants security, especially financial security.

RABBI: Lack of financial security in a marriage can certainly add tremendous strain to a marriage; conversely, money in the house can cover up a lot of problems. Nevertheless, I would not say that money is the most important thing.

SHAINA: Rabbi, a woman needs love. She needs to feel loved.

RABBI: You call it love, but I would like to define love more specifically and call it attention, *simas laiv*. If the woman feels that the husband really cares about her, then she will be the happiest person in the world. If she does not have that feeling, then whatever he gives her is not enough.

Let's look into this. There are many things that can trigger an argument in a household. A husband comes home one day from work and his wife is crying.

"Why are you crying?" he asks.

"Because," she says, "in the morning I told you to remember to take out the garbage." The garbage, though, wasn't really what bothered her, so from there she proceeds to enumerate a list of everything he has not been doing for her. Invariably, the last thing she says to him is, "You really don't care for me. You really don't love me."

A man has to realize that his wife needs his attention. She has a built-in need to feel that he thinks about her during his day.

MOSHE: Rabbi, doesn't a man need attention as well?

RABBI: Yes, however, I would say that for a man the most important thing is not attention, but *kavod,* honor. More than anything, a man needs respect; to be shown that he is important.

You can see this difference between a man's and a woman's needs in the thought processes when they go to buy clothing.

What does a woman who buys clothes look for? She wants the attention of others. If she is a modest, Torah-observant woman she stands in front of the mirror and says to herself, "Is my husband going to like me in this dress?" She wants him to shower his affection on her because of it. She wants his attention.

Often when a woman goes shopping she will buy five dresses with the intention of returning the three or four that her husband does not like best on her. She brings them home because she wants his approval. After trying them all on for him she asks, "What do you think?"

"It doesn't matter to me," he says. "Buy any one you want. If you want to do me a favor, buy the *cheapest* dress."

The problem is not only that he just did the worst thing he can do to his wife, but he probably thinks he is a *tzaddik* because he is not interested in material things.

The man is making a big mistake if he takes this attitude. He doesn't understand that she wants his input. She has a need to find favor in his eyes. The way he can please her most is if he shows a real interest in which dress she buys. That is the most important thing to a woman. If she feels that he cares about her, everything else is secondary. If she is missing that, everything is meaningless.

Now, when a man goes to buy a suit he does not say to himself, "Am I going to be attractive to my wife in this suit?" Instead, he looks in the mirror and says to himself, "Do I look respectable in this suit?" He views his clothes as a measure of his stature in society. Even if he wears old blue jeans to show how uninterested in

stature he is, he still does so in order to make a
statement to society that he is casual.

The most important thing to a man is to feel that his
wife sees him as someone who has worth, who is
respected. These attitudes, in fact, are *halachic*
obligations. The Rambam writes that a woman should
view her husband like a king.[61] For women, the Sages
say that a man has to love his wife as himself and give
her respect even more than himself.[62]

SHAINA: Why is that?

MOSHE: Yes. What is the underlying idea behind these
laws?

RABBI: Man's need for honor and respect is rooted in
the curse *Hashem* decreed upon Adam: "By the sweat
of your brow you shall eat bread."[63] This in effect
forced Adam to labor for his bread. Coming from the
Garden of Eden, this was very demeaning to him.
Therefore, he became dependent on his wife Chava to
rebuild his ego. So, too, today when men go out into
the world and work for a living they meet with
frustration, disappointment, and individuals who seek
to cut them down in size in the hope of thereby
gaining an advantage. That is one motivation, then,
behind the law requiring a wife to have additional
respect for her husband.

Similarly, a woman's need for love and attention is
rooted in the curse that Chava received, "In pain shall
you bear children; and your desire shall be for your

husband."[64] Pregnancy and even a woman's monthly cycle take her through highs and lows which intensify her need for attention. Therefore, a husband is commanded to love his wife as himself and to take care of her needs more than his own.

By fulfilling their respective duties to the other partner, each couple negates and even turns into a positive force, the fall-out caused by the curse on Adam and Chava.

The Heart Follows the Action

Now, if both spouses fulfilled their respective obligations all would be fine. The problem is that each party usually wants the other one to fulfill his or her obligations.

The woman comes to a rabbi and says, "Rabbi, my *shalom bayis* is in shambles."

"Why is it in shambles?" he asks.

"Very simple," she says. "The Sages say that a man must love his wife as he loves himself, and respect her more than himself. And my husband is so self-centered, he can't love anyone more than himself. That is why we have no *shalom bayis*."

The rabbi then calls in the husband. "What seems to be the problem?"

"Rabbi," he says, "the problem is very simple. The Rambam writes that a woman is supposed to treat her husband like a king, and my wife treats me like a rag. She steps all over me every chance she gets. How could there possibly be *shalom bayis*?"

The real problem is that each of them sees only what the other is obligated to give. They do not see their obligation to the other.

MOSHE: But, let's say they really don't feel the way they are obligated to feel about each other.

RABBI: That's a good question.

SHAINA: Can you repeat it?

RABBI: In other words, let's say, for instance, that the husband says, "I know it is written that a man is supposed to love his wife as much as himself, and respect her more than himself, but I like myself a thousand times more than I like her. She is a fine person who takes care of the house and the children, but I don't have strong feelings towards her."

She, in turn, says, "Yes, the Rambam rules that a wife should view her husband as a king. Maybe the Rambam's wife was able to view the Rambam as a king, but my husband is not the Rambam."

MOSHE: What are they supposed to do in that situation?

SHAINA: Are they supposed to fake it?

RABBI: The author of the *Sefer HaChinuch* writes a fundamental principle: "The heart follows the action."[65] In other words, a person's outward acts affect his or her inner thoughts and feelings.

By way of illustration, which would you say is better

for the person who decides that in order to overcome selfishness he vows to give a million dollars to charity? Should he give the million dollars away all at one time? Or should he give a dollar one million times?

MOSHE: I don't know.

RABBI: He should give one dollar a million times because each act of giving a dollar awakens and fans the instinct to be charitable.

Now, if a man says about his wife, "I know that I don't like her as I like myself." And she says, "My husband is no king." In that event, they can still say to themselves, "Despite what I know to be the truth, I will go through the motions."

Specifically, the woman says to herself about the husband, "From now on he is going to be a king to me. If he comes home at seven o'clock, then by five to seven I will have supper on the table; I'm going to use the nicest silverware; I'll put a doily under his grapefruit plate; the house is going to be in order; I'm going to dress nicely and ask him what I can do for him; I'm going to treat him like a king."

In turn, the husband says about his wife, "No matter what I really feel, in the middle of the day I am going to call her up, and ask her how everything is; when I come home I am going to ask her how the day went; I am going to take an interest in the household; if she moved a flowerpot to a different end of the window sill I will say, 'I think it looks well in this corner,' even if I don't really care; I will make positive comments if she puts a new tablecloth on the table or is wearing a special dress. I am going to make believe we are going out again."

If the couple does that faithfully, they will come to really feel about the other what they are performing on the outside. The negatives which they saw in each other for even ten or twenty years will diminish. If they follow this program, even if it is a little artificial in the beginning, slowly their relationship will improve. "The heart follows the action."

The Most Detrimental Character Trait

Time is running late; there is only so much we can cover in one session. Before we leave, however, let me ask you the following: What would you say is the most detrimental character trait that a person can bring into a household?

SHAINA: I think I once heard someone say sadness.

RABBI: That's a very good guess. The Chazon Ish in fact writes in one of his letters that a *bais medrash*-type seriousness has almost no place in the household. A husband who is always long-faced and sulking is inappropriate, especially since he probably thinks he is a *tzaddik for* fulfilling the commandment to mourn over the *chorbon Bais Hamikdash,* the destruction of the Temple. Even so, I would say that there is something more detrimental to a peaceful home.

MOSHE: Anger.

RABBI: I think most people would agree with you that anger is the biggest tension builder in a household. I too agree. Nevertheless, in order to get to the root of the problem we have to ask: Where does anger stem from? The answer is that anger comes from *gaavah*, conceit. A person only becomes angry with others because he is self-centered.

MOSHE: How's that?

RABBI: It is the nature of a person to feel that he is perfect. Therefore, when he sees imperfection in someone else it really irritates him because he says to himself, "I would never do something like that."

Let me illustrate it for you. I grew up in a city and was trained by my parents from childhood to always lock the door. However, my wife grew up in the suburbs where no one took such precautions. When I married, I tried to instill into my wife and children the habit of always checking to see if the doors and windows were locked. Nevertheless, the children picked up their mother's habit despite my constant reminders and exhortations to always lock up.

One morning, on my way out of the house, I saw that the door was unlocked. This was the last straw. I turned around and began walking toward the children's bedroom to see who was the last one out of the house the previous night. Whoever it was, was really going to get scolded.

As I began walking toward their room, however, I slowly reminded myself that the last one out of the house the previous night was none other than me. I had gone to get the mail, and, preoccupied with reading it, I came back in forgetting to lock the door.

Do you think I turned the anger toward myself? No. In that second I said to myself, "These things happen. People forget."

The point is that a person naturally loves himself very much. In fact, he loves himself so much that it covers all other shortcomings. If we had just a percentage of that love of ourselves for others then we would not get angry.

The Most Desirable Character Trait

MOSHE: If conceit is the worst, then what is the most ideal character trait that a person can bring into a household?

SHAINA: I would say patience.

RABBI: Patience is desirable, however, a patient person can nevertheless always have a sullen, solemn look. There may be lack of conflict in that home, but I don't think anyone would say that the silence in that case is healthy. No, patience alone will not create the ideal atmosphere.

SHAINA: Then what will?

RABBI: To me it seems that more than any other character trait, *simcha* — happiness, contentment, satisfaction, optimism, the feeling that things are going well — is the most important trait anyone can bring into a marriage.

SHAINA: What makes *simcha* so special?

RABBI: Because it is contagious; it can infuse others with the same feeling, and override all the difficulties in a relationship. The great benefit of this character trait for a marriage is that it can change a household even if only one spouse exhibits it. Of course, if both parties express this trait all the better.

MOSHE: But, rabbi, sometimes a person really has a lousy day. What is he supposed to do then?

RABBI: To be happy when things go well is easy. However, to possess the character trait of *simcha,* one has to work on oneself to exhibit it independent of external events. The author of the *Chovos Halevavos* describes the ideal person as one whose "face radiates *simcha,* even though his pain is in his heart."

Let's talk about it practically in terms of a day-to-day situation in the average home. Say a husband walks into a house and his wife asks him how his day went. If it wasn't one of his better days, he might say, "What a miserable day! The traffic was bad enough, but the car almost overheated. I had to turn off the air conditioner. It's only four years old, and we still haven't finished the payments on it, but we need a new car. I am sick and tired of it. That's how my day went."

In that first minute he already set the tone for the remainder of the evening.

MOSHE: How else can he come in if that's the situation, though?

RABBI: He can say the exact same words in a funny, light-hearted way. "What kind of a day did I have? Terrific! *Gevaldig*! Fantastic! My air conditioner broke down, the car is ready for the junkyard. What a wonderful day!"

What he accomplished with this is that he let off some steam in a positive way and set an upbeat tone for the evening. Later, without the additional tension of stress between husband and wife, he can deal with his aggravation.

The same thing is true for the wife. He comes home and asks her how her day was.

"You really want to know?" she says. "It was miserable. I took the kids to the doctor; I had to wait an hour; he wanted me to pay; I didn't have a check. I was embarrassed because last month our check bounced. I'm miserable; I can't handle it any longer!"

If that's the response he got for his, "Hello, I'm home," then you can imagine how the rest of the night is going to go.

On the other hand she could have said, "What an unbelievable day. I took the kids to the doctor; I had to wait for an hour; he wanted me to pay on the spot;

I didn't have a check. It was fantastic!" If her tone is right she can break all the tension.

I'm not telling you to deny your true feelings and never share them with your spouse. However, when you first come home and both of you are aware of the tensions and stresses in your lives, train yourselves in the character trait of *simcha.* It will only help you ultimately deal better with the other problems because a positive, healthy relationship between a husband and wife is the most important thing. Everything else is bearable if you have that. The smallest things are unbearable if you don't.

Well, it is late. Just remember this last thing and take it home with you. "When a man and women are worthy, the Divine Presence dwells among them."[66] If a man knows how to go home and say thank you; and if a woman knows how to greet him, then the Divine Presence dwells among them.

MOSHE: Rabbi, I appreciate your taking time and talking with us. I've already found it very helpful — especially the advice about the *shanah rishonah.*

SHAINA: Me too. I think we know what we have to work on now.

RABBI: You can call me whenever you want. We discussed a lot of the general principles tonight; from now on we will have a framework to understand the specific things that crop up. At least call me in couple of weeks to hear how things are progressing.

APPENDICES

Appendix A:
Sayings of the Sages for Men and Women

When a soul is sent down from heaven, it contains both male and female characteristics; the male part enters the baby boy, and the female, the baby girl; and if they are worthy, *Hashem* reunites them in marriage (*Zohar Tazria* 43b).

Forty days before the creation of a child, a voice proclaims in heaven: So and so's daughter is for so and so (*Sota* 2a).

Rabbah once overheard a man praying that a certain woman should become his wife. Rabbah reproved him, saying, "If she is the right woman for you, she will not be kept from you; if she is not, then your unanswered prayer might cause you to lose faith in *Hashem*" (*Moed Katan* 18b).

The relationship of husband to wife is like the relationship of the right hand to the left hand (Letters of the Chazon Ish).

The Hebrew words for man — *ish* (spelled *aleph, yud, shin*) — and woman — *ishah* (spelled *aleph, shin, hey*) — are three letter words which share two common letters (*aleph* and *shin*) and one letter unique to each (the *yud* of *ish,* and the *hey* of *ishah).* Together, the *yud* and the *hey* spell *Hashem*'s name. Therefore, the job of man and woman is to utilize their unique letters of holiness and reunite them. If they do not bring the *yud* and the *hey* into their relationship — if they do not make the focus of their relationship the goal of spiritual, soul reunion — then all that remains is the *aleph* and *shin* of *ish* plus the *aleph* and *shin* of *ishah; aleph* and *shin* spell *aish,* fire. In other words, husband and wife lacking the goal of spiritual union, like two consuming fires, will destroy each other (*Sota* 17b).

"Whenever there is peace in a house, it is as if there is peace in the entire world" (*Avos d'Rabi Nosson*). The home is where everything starts.

Every Jewish home represents the Tabernacle. If the man and wife are worthy, the *Shechinah,* the Divine Presence, is there just as it was in the Tabernacle (*Sota* 17a).

"The world is built on giving (*chesed*)." *Chesed* is the foundation of a Jewish home.

In the fifth chapter of *Devarim, Hashem* acknowledges how well His people listened and revered Him at the giving of the Torah by Mount Sinai. Then He tells Moshe, "Go, say to them, 'Return to your tents'"

(Deuteronomy 5:27), as if to say, "Now let's see how well your reverence and attachment to Me manifest themselves in your private lives, in your households (Rebbe of Kotsk).

When love is strong, a man and a woman can make their bed on a sword's blade; when love is weak, a bed of sixty measures is not wide enough (*Sanhedrin* 7a).

If love depends on something, when the "something" ceases, the love ceases. If love does not depend on anything, then it never ceases (*Avos* 5:19).

Be especially on guard Friday afternoon, before the onset of *Shabbos,* about getting into an argument. The forces of evil are particularly active at that time, trying to induce husband and wife to get angry at each other. It is precisely at that time that husband and wife have to be extra conscious to embrace the trait of peace between themselves (Chidah, *Moreh B'Etzbah,* page 140).

"The words of the wise, in gentleness are heard" (*Koheles* 9:17). A person should never think that raising his voice makes him heard better. On the contrary, it only motivates opposition.

When difficulties arise and husband and wife get into a fight, the laws of *loshon hara* (malicious speech) and *rechilus* (tale-bearing) are still very much in force. If you relay information about your spouse to your friends or relatives, you are not free to say whatever you want. The best solution is to avoid revealing anything negative about your spouse to anyone who would naturally side with you. Rather, both spouses should seek out a single third party who can hear them out and remain as impartial as possible. In that case, if the information has some positive purpose, it would be permissible to reveal the details of the disagreement. In all other circumstances, it is best to not say anything which may even only approach the serious transgressions of *loshon hara* or *rechilus*.

"As water reflects one face to another face, so too, is one heart to another heart" (Proverbs 27:19). What one spouse feels about another, the other feels. If you view your spouse positively, he or she will view you positively. If you view your spouse negatively, he or she will harbor the same feelings about you.

"From the very beginning of creation, *Hashem* is 'busy' pairing couples." Serving *Hashem* can only be fulfilled if the goal is to unite opposites (Maharal, *Be'er HaGaola*, p. 83). The greatest accomplishment in this world is taking opposites and uniting them.

In the natural state, the body's needs compete with the

soul's needs — this is what makes marriage so challenging. However, this is also why fulfillment of self can only occur through marriage. Only where there is so much at stake can so much be gained.

The purpose of life is to fuse the body to the soul, and that only occurs when the person learns to harness the needs of the body for the use of the soul. There are those who appear happy in marriage; the truth is, though, that in many cases they are only happy because they have not even taken up the challenge of trying to harness the body's desires for the uses of the soul. They have not even begun fulfilling their purpose in life.

Only through the challenge of marriage can a person hope to eliminate selfishness.

"No man is successful in Torah unless he first stumbles in it" (*Gittin* 71). Similarly, there is no successful marriage which begins without difficulties.

A woman asks for gratification in her heart; the man with his mouth (*Eruvin* 100b).

It is easier to appease a male than a female since Adam was created from dust [which is soft], but Chava was created out of bone [which is hard] (*Niddah* 31b).

Of all *mitzvos* which can be classified as "between person and person" (*bain udum l'chaveiro*), your relationship to your spouse takes priority in all respects. There are many Torah statements and commandments in which this applies: 1) "Love your friend as you love yourself" starts at home. If you have a choice between giving either only to a neighbor or only to your spouse, your spouse comes first. 2) In the first year of marriage, giving priority to your wife is even greater, as we are especially commanded to "make your wife happy" in that first year. 3) The Torah has a unique commandment, "Judge your people righteously." This is the idea of *limud zechus*, judging favorably. There is no one closer among "your people" than your spouse. Because living so close to each other can cause more friction, there is an even greater obligation to look only for the positive. 4) Another Torah commandment is the obligation to "Go in His way" — to imitate *Hashem*. Just as *Hashem* is merciful, so should we; just as *Hashem* holds back anger, so to speak, so should we. This applies even more so in a marital relationship. 5) "Don't hate your brother in your heart." Your wife is an even closer relative than a brother. Sometimes, silence in a home can be more devastating than anything else. 6) On the other hand, "Don't hurt each other with words." Be very careful in what you say and the way you say it, if and when it is necessary to say something you are harboring inside. 7) "Don't spread rumors." Never carry your anger to the point where you include negative statements about your spouse's family. 8) "Don't seek revenge."

There is a substitute for everything except the wife of one's youth (*Sanhedrin* 22a).

A second marriage is much more difficult than the first. If people would only invest into the first marriage a third of the effort they would have to invest in a second marriage, the first marriage will end up better than the second could ever be.

"*Hashem* settles individuals in the house; He frees prisoners with ropes [*b'cho'shoros*]" (Psalms 68:7). *Chazal* (*Beraishis Rabbah* 68:4) seek the deeper meaning of the verse and interpret: Who are the "individuals"? A husband and wife. How are they freed from the prison of self implied by calling them "individuals"? Through "*b'cho'shoros*," meaning "sometimes through crying ("*b'cho*" related to *bechi*) and sometimes through song" ("*shoros*" related to *shir*]. Sometimes a marriage is very painful; sometimes it goes relatively smoothly. In either case, it is *Hashem*'s way of bringing each member of the couple to completion.

Hashem is in charge of everything, and He has a reason even for the pairing up of one spouse who has a problem with another who doesn't.

Divorce is an amputation.

Tears fall on *Hashem*'s altar whenever divorce occurs"
(*Gittin* 90a). The altar is a symbol of connection between
us and our Father in heaven. When husband and wife
separate, there is a parallel separation between the
congregation of Israel and *Hashem*.

Marriage is a forum for ongoing, continuous growth.

"The purpose of life is to break your bad character
traits; if not, what else is there?" (Vilna Gaon, *Evven
Shlaimah*).

"Sanctify yourself and be holy." Sanctify yourself down
here just a little, and you will be sanctified a lot from
above. Sanctify yourself in this world, and you will be
sanctified in the world-to-come (*Yoma* 39).

"Be holy" (*Vayikra* 19:2). Sanctify yourself even in things
the Torah permits you. Don't be a repulsive person with
the permission of the Torah (Ramban).

"The Egyptians forced the Israelites to work with cruelty
(*b'pharech*)" (*Shmos* 1:13). What does with cruelty
(*b'pharech*) mean? They forced the women to do men's
labor, and the men to do women's labor (*Sota* 11). We
see that it is very important for man and woman not to

exchange roles.

"And they said to him, 'Where is your wife?' And he replied, 'She is in the tent'" (Genesis 18:9). The angels knew that Sarah remained in her tent due to her modesty, nevertheless they asked Abraham her whereabouts in order to remind him of his wife's modesty, which would further endear her to him (*Bava Metziah* 87a).

Rabbi Meir said, "Why did the Torah make her a *niddah* for seven days? Because, when he becomes accustomed to her, he might come to despise her. Therefore, the Torah said she should remain unclean for seven days, so that she should be endeared to her husband as at the time of her coming under the wedding canopy" (*Niddah* 31b).

Appendix B:
Sayings of the Sages for Men

A good wife is a gift from heaven, and is given to one who fears *Hashem* (*Yevamos* 63b).

He who finds a wife, finds good (Proverbs 18:22). The man alone is not yet *tov* (good). Completion of the *tov* only comes through marriage. And the only way for the *tov* to become complete is by following the instructions (Torah) of the One who created man, woman, and *tov*.

The king asked Rabban Gamliel, "Your G-d is a thief because He put Adam to sleep and then stole one of his ribs!" At this the king's daughter said to her father, "Call the guard!" "Why? What happened?" he asked. She said, "A thief broke into my house, took a silver pitcher and left a gold one in its place." The king replied, "If only such a thief would do that to me!" Thereupon the daughter responded, "Was it not also better that Adam had a rib taken from him only to be replaced by a wife?" (*Sanhedrin* 39a).

It is natural for a man to seek a woman, and not the reverse, because the loser seeks what he has lost (*Niddah* 31b).

A man without a wife lives without joy, blessing, good

. . . and Torah (*Yevamos* 62b).

A woman is the essence of the home. Rabbi Yosi said, I never call her, "my wife"; I call her "my home" (*Shabbos* 118b).

"It is good for a man in his youth to carry a yoke" (*Eichah* 3:27). What is the yoke? The yoke of Torah, and the yoke of a wife . . . (*Eichah Rabbah* 3:9).

A man should always be careful with the honor of his wife, because blessing comes to a home only through her (*Bava Metziah* 59).

It is not possible for a man to be without a wife, and togetherness cannot be achieved without the *Shechinah,* the Divine Presence (*Beraishis Rabbah* 3:18). The *Shechinah* only dwells in a place where man dwells with his wife (*Zohar Beraishis* 122).

A man without a wife is not a man, as the Torah says (Genesis 5:2): "Male and female He created them, and He called their names [plural] Man (Adam)" (*Yevamos* 63).

A man is not called a man until he is united with woman (*Zohar Vayikra* 5b). A man without a wife is not complete (*Zohar Hazinu* 296). If a man never marries, it would be better had he never been born (*Evven HaEzer* 2). A man without a wife has no defense against temptation (*Yevamos* 63a). When a man marries, his sins decrease (*Kiddushin* 29b).

The first year of marriage is especially important for laying the foundation of later years, and, as such, has special status. The man should be available to his wife for the full year in order to gain an understanding of her nature and needs for the sake of making her happy and coming to love her more. He should forget what he learned about all other women in the world, and find out what her needs are (*Sefer HaChinuch* 582).

A woman prefers poverty with love to riches without love (*Yerushalmi Sota* 3:4).

Who makes the wife happy? Her husband (*Rosh HaShannah* 6b).

The primary wish of a woman is to have a husband who loves her and cares for her. If she suspects this is not so, it is almost as if her life is in danger (*pikuach nefesh*). A great pain and sadness overcome her as if she were a widow (Steipler Rav).

When Abraham moved to the mountain east of Bais El and pitched his tent, the word for tent (*oholo*) is used with the feminine suffix. This teaches that Abraham first pitched Sarah's tent and then his own, which demonstrates caring for his wife's needs first (Rashi, Genesis 12:8).

Love your wife as yourself and honor her more (*Yevamos* 62b).

The Sages commanded a man to respect his wife more than he respects himself. In addition, he has to love his wife as he loves himself. If he has a lot of money, he should spend it for her benefit. He should never impose excessive fear. He should speak to her pleasantly. There should not be sadness or anger detected in his words (Rambam, *Ishus* 15:19).

A man should always eat, drink and dress less than he can afford. However, with regard to these matters concerning his wife and children, he should spend more than he can afford (*Chullin* 84).

Included in the positive commandment for a man to feed his wife is the obligation to take care of all her personal, daily needs (*Ra'avad*).

Included in the man's obligation to respect his wife is the buying of jewelry and clothes (Rashi, *Sanhedrin* 76b).

Whenever a man leaves the house he should tell his wife where he is going. When he returns he should tell her what he did. Include her even in things which seem small to you in order to make her happy (Letters of the Chazon Ish).

Every man needs to be especially careful to avoid hurting his wife with words, because "her tears are near," i.e., she cries more easily (*Bava Metziah* 59).

A woman feels embarrassment more than a man. Therefore, if an embarrassing situation arises, the man should steer the embarrassing situation to himself (*Yevamos* 62b).

Always consult with and incorporate your wife in your decision-making. When Rabbi Elazar ben Azariah was asked to become leader of the entire Jewish world, he said that first he had to consult with his wife (*Berachos* 27b).

Hashem gave women extra wisdom (*binah*) (*Niddah* 45).

A man should respect his wife's opinion in all worldly matters. "If your wife is short, bend down in order to hear her advice" (*Bava Metziah* 59).

Telling your wife that the soup was delicious is like

telling your *Rosh Yeshiva* that his solution to *Tosafos* was especially brilliant (Rabbi Yisrael Salanter).

Adam's sleep during the creation of Chava teaches that a husband should sometimes act as if he is asleep and unaware of his wife's shortcomings. He should overlook faults to avoid domestic quarrels (*Toldos Yitzchak*).

A man may flatter his wife for the sake of domestic tranquility (*Otzair Midrashim* 224).

Three charms exist: [One is] the charm of a wife to her husband (*Sota* 47) even if she is unattractive (Rashi).

The wife of Rav Chiyah did her best to always annoy and anger him. Nevertheless, whenever he could find something nice to buy he would purchase it for her. Rav, the disciple of Rav Chiyah, asked him why he always bought her such nice gifts. "It's enough if they only raise our children and rescue us from sin" (*Yevamos* 63).

Before a man marries, his love goes to his parents; after he marries, it goes to his wife (*Pirkei d'Rabi Eliezer* 32).

He who looks for the earnings of his wife never sees a sign of blessing (*Pesachim* 50b).

"Descend a step and marry a woman" (*Yevamos* 63).

Appendix C:
Sayings of the Sages for Women

Charm is empty and beauty is vain; a woman who fears *Hashem*, she shall be praised (Proverbs 31:30).

We learn fear of sin from the woman who prayed, "May it be Your will *Hashem* that no man stumbles because of me" (*Sota* 22). She was praying that men shouldn't stare at her and come to sin.

The glory of the king's daughter is inside (Psalms 45:14).

A gold ring in a pig's nose — so a pretty woman without sense (Proverbs 11:22).

A wife is the joy of a man's heart (*Shabbos* 152a).

A good wife is a crown to her husband; but one who acts shamefully is like rot in his bones (Proverbs 12:4).

A good wife, who can find? Far above rubies is her worth; her husband trusts in her. Her children grow up and call her blessed (Proverbs 31:10).

How great is the virtuous woman, for the Torah itself is compared to her (*Yevamos* 63).

In his home, every man is king (*Avos d'Rabbi Nosson* 28). A wise woman told her daughter, "Serve your husband as a king. If you will act toward him like his maid, he will act toward you as a servant and honor you like a queen. But if you try to dominate him, he will be your master and you will be in his eyes as a maidservant" (*Menoras haMoaor, Ner* 3 chapter 2).

A woman should respect her husband greatly, and accord him reverence. She should fulfill his requests, and consider him like a minister or king. This is the manner of the daughters of Israel who are holy and pure, building their marriage to the point where they have happy, tranquil family members (Rambam, *Ishus* 15:20).

Who is an upright (*kosher*) woman? The one who performs the desire of her husband (*Tana d'bei Eliyahu* 9).

Who is a woman of valor? The one who unlearns her parents' customs and learns her husband's, to the point where she can almost be called the daughter of her husband rather than the daughter of her father. This is where the societal custom of women dropping the name of their father's family upon marriage and taking up the name of their husband's family arose (Meiri, *Mishlei* 31).

The woman was told, "And he shall rule over you"

(Genesis 3:16). The man should be the leader because he symbolizes mercy (*rachamim*) while she symbolizes justice (*din*). If the man leads, the household is judged from above with mercy; however, if the woman leads, then the household is judged from above according to the scales of strict justice (Chidah, *Sefer Bamidbar Kedeimos* 5:15).

Greater is the guarantee *Hashem* gave women than he gave to men, as it says, "Women of peace, get up; listen to my voice, you confident builders" (Isaiah 32:9). They have a greater guarantee of peace in this world, and can be confident about their portion in the world-to-come (*Berachos* 17).

"So shall you say to the house of Jacob, and declare to the children of Israel" (Exodus 19:3). The "house of Jacob" is a reference to the women. *Hashem* singles them out and tells Moses here to speak to them softly (Rashi) because their reward is greater than the men's (Maharal, *Derashos Al HaTorah* 27).

How do women gain a portion in the reward of learning Torah? They take their children to the schools to learn, and wait for their husbands to return from learning Torah in yeshiva (*Berachos* 17).

Rabbi Akiva commissioned a jeweler to make an

expensive piece of jewelry for his wife (which he had promised her when they lived in poverty). When the wife of Rabban Gamliel (who had always lived in wealth) saw it, she became envious. He told her, "Did you do for me what she did for her husband, selling tresses of her hair so he could devote himself to Torah?" (*Yerushalmi, Shabbos* 6:1).

The wife of Abba Chilkiah would always greet her husband dressed in her finest clothes and wearing perfume to make sure that her husband would not look at any other woman (*Taanis* 24).

The woman who does not adorn herself for her husband brings evil upon herself (Hai Gaon).

Thrift, soft-heartedness and naivete are virtues in a woman (*Chasdai b. Hamelech Vehanazir*).

It is a woman's nature to be more compassionate than a man (Rashi, *Melachim* 2:22).

More than man desires to marry, woman desires to be married (*Yevamos* 113a).

A certain woman used to attend Rabbi Meir's Friday night class. Once, the class took longer than usual, and she came home very late. Her husband, infuriated, demanded an explanation. Even though she explained, he told her, "I won't let you back in the house until you spit in Rabbi Meir's face!" Rabbi Meir found out about the woman's dilemma. Pretending that something had fallen in his eye, he asked her to spit in his eye seven times. After doing so, Rabbi Meir said to her, "Go, tell your husband that you did more than what was asked of you." Rabbi Meir's disciples, angered by the husband's disrespect toward their teacher, said to Rabbi Meir, "If we had known the situation, we would have beaten him up." Rabbi Meir replied, "Meir's honor should not be greater than his Creator's honor. The Torah states that even the sacred name of *Hashem* is erased in water to make peace between husband and wife. All the more so should I forgo my honor" (*Bamidbar Rabbah* 9:19).

A woman, who is modest in her home, brings atonement for her household as the altar brought atonement for Israel (*Tanchuma VaYishlach* 6).

A woman who roams the marketplace conversing with every man, brings evil upon herself and her children (*Tana d'bei Eliyahu Rabbah* 18).

After they were divorced, the man married a bad woman and she made him bad; the woman married a bad man and she made him good. This proves that all depends on the woman (*Beraishis Rabbah* 17:12).

Appendix D:
Recommended Reading List

Aizer K'negdo; Sarah Radcliffe; Distributed by Feldheim.*

Bayis Ne'eman B'Yisroel; Rabbi Meir Wikler; Distributed by Feldheim.*

Fulfillment In Marriage, 2 Vols.; Rabbi Shmuel D. Eisenblatt; Distributed by Feldheim.*

In Search Of The Jewish Woman; Rabbi Yisroel Miller; Distributed by Feldheim.*

Shidduchim & Zivugim; Rabbi Yehudah Lebovits; Distributed by Feldheim.*

The Jew And His Home; Rabbi Eliyahu Ki Tov; Shengold Publishers 45 West 45th St. NY NY 10036.

The Secret of Jewish Femininity: Insights into the Practice of Taharat HaMishpacha (Family Purity Laws); Tehilla Abramov; Distributed by Feldheim.

The Waters of Eden; Rabbi Aryeh Kaplan; Distributed by NCSY/OU 45 West 36th St., NY NY 10018.

The River, The Kettle, And The Bird; Rabbi Aharon Feldman; Distributed by Feldheim.*

* Philip Feldheim Inc., 200 Airport Executive Park, Spring Valley, NY 10977, (914) 356-2282/(800) 237-7149.

GLOSSARY

BAAL TESHUVA (BAALES TESHUVA f.): A person who deepens his/her commitment to Judaism through a "return" to Torah observance.

BAIS HAMIKDASH: The Temple in Jerusalem (the second of which was destroyed by the Romans in 70 C.E.).

BAIS MEDRASH: The house of learning (in a *yeshiva*).

BASHERT: "The intended."

BORUCH HASHEM: Blessed is G-d; thank G-d.

CHALAL: Hollow, a void.

CHAVA: Eve (the wife of Adam).

CHAZAL (pl.): Hebrew abbreviation for "The Sages (of the oral Torah) of blessed memory."

CHERUBIM (pl.): The golden figures on the ark, which itself was situated in the *Kodesh HaKadoshim*.

CHESED: Giving, loving-kindness, altruism.

CHILLUL HASHEM: Desecration of G-d's name.

CHOK: A statute (usually in reference to one which is beyond human reasoning, as opposed to many civil laws which immediately make sense to the human mind).

GEMILUS CHASADIM: See *chesed*.

GOY KADOSH: Holy nation.

HALACHA: Jewish law.

HASHEM: G-d; literally, "The Name."

HASHKAFA: (Torah) outlook.

KIDDUSH HASHEM: Sanctification of G-d's name.

KODESH HAKADOSHIM: The Holy of Holies; the innermost chamber of the Temple (as opposed to the *Kodesh*, or Holy, and the *Ulam*, or entranceway). One had to first enter the *Ulam* to get to the *Kodesh* (which housed the *menorah*, incense altar and *shulchan*-table); and one could only reach the Holy of Holies through first passing through the *Kodesh*. Only the *Kohen Gadol* entered the Holy of Holies, and he did so only once a year on Yom Kippur.

KOHEN GADOL: The High Priest. (See *Kohen*.)

KOHEN: A descendant of Aaron, who was assigned performance of the Temple rituals when the Temple stood.

MENORAH: The special seven-pronged candelabrum in the

Temple.

MESECHTA: A single volume, or tractate, of the *Talmud*.

MISHNA: The pithy statements of Jewish law upon which *Talmudic* discussion is centered.

MITZVAH (MITZVOS pl.): A commandment. The written Torah enumerates 613 — 248 positive commandments and 365 negative commandments.

MITZVAS ASAY SHEHAZMAN GRAMA: Literally, "positive commandments (as opposed to negative commandments ['you shall not'] that time causes." For example, "You shall take" the esrog-fruit and lulav-branch on the festival of Succos (Lev. 23.40).

MITZVOS: See *Mitzvah*.

NEFESH BEHAMIS: The animal soul.

NESHAMA: Soul (usually in reference to the higher, more spiritual soul).

OVED HASHEM: A servant of G-d.

SHADCHAN: A matchmaker.

SHALOM BAYIS: A peaceful home environment.

SHANAH RISHONAH: The first year (of marriage).

SHECHINAH: The Divine Presence.

SHEVA BERACHOS: (Literally, "the seven blessings".) The week of festivities following a Jewish wedding.

SHIDDUCH: A match (see *shadchan*).

SIMCHA: Joy, happiness.

T'FILLEN: Black boxes made in accordance with Jewish law, worn by men on the head and arm, usually during morning services.

TAHARAS HAMISHPACHA: Family purity laws.

TALMID CHACHAM: A Torah scholar.

TALMUD: The oral Torah, transmitted first by G-d to Moses at Mount Sinai and then transmitted down through the generations until persecution warranted its being written in the form of the *Mishna*, which itself (some three centuries later) needed to be explained and elaborated upon through the words of the *Talmud*. The *Talmud,* then, is the written record of the "oral" Torah, G-d transmitted to Moses.

TIKUN: A "repair."

TORAH: Scripture (the written Torah) and *Talmud* (the oral Torah) comprising the source and essence of Judaism.

TOV: Good.

TZADDIK: A righteous man.

TZEDEYKUS: A righteous woman.

TZELEM ELOKIM: The image of G-d.

TZITZIS: "Fringes" which the Torah commands be put on four-cornered garments.

TZNIYUS: Literally, modesty.

YESHIVA: A school for teaching Torah.

YICHUD *ROOM*: The room where the couple goes directly after the ceremony under the wedding canopy to be alone.

REFERENCES

1. Commentary on *Beraishis* (Genesis) 1:1.
2. *Beraishis* 2:18. [The conventional translation is: It is not good for man to be alone. However, see the section (ahead) entitled Being The Man Alone for the rationale behind our rendering of this verse.]
3. *Moed Katan* 18b.
4. *The River, the Kettle, and the Bird*, pp. 32-33.
5. *Gittin* 90a.
6. *Zohar, Beraishis* 122.
7. *Sota* 17b.
8. [See Appendices A, B, C.]
9. *Beraishis* 1:26.
10. [First initials of *Rabbi Moshe ben Nachman*, also known as Nachmanides.]
11. Cf. *Kuzari*. [See the section entitled Oved Hashem.]
12. *Beraishis* 2:7.
13. Isaiah 57:16.
14. *Derech Hashem* 1.
15. See *Michtav M'Eliyahu,* Vol. 1.
16. *Avos* 4:2.
17. See Rashi, *Beraishis* 12:11.
18. *Beraishis* 1:27.
19. See also *Beraishis* 5:1,2.
20. Compare to *Tehillim* (Psalms) 29.
21. *Vayikra* (Leviticus) 19:18.
22. Rambam, *Ishus* 15:19.
23. *Yevamos* 62b.
24. [The following account is actually told over by Rabbi Yisrael Rokowsky, Rosh Yeshiva Ohr Somayach, Monsey, New York.]
25. *Bava Metziah* 59.
26. *Beraishis* 2:18.
27. *Avos* 1:13.
28. *Devarim* (Deuteronomy) 30:19.
29. *Gittin* 71.
30. *Yoma* 39.
31. *Beraishis* 1:26.
32. *Zohar, Tazria* 43b.

33. *Sota* 2a.
34. [See above, the section entitled Oved Hashem for the background information to this and other points brought up in the ensuing discussion.]
35. *Zohar Beraishis* 2:4.
36. Isaiah 41:8.
37. *Zohar.*
38. *Niddah* 31.
39. *Niddah* 31b.
40. *Ohr Yitzchak (M'Radvil), parshas Terumah.*
41. *Shmos* (Exodus) 25:22.
42. *Beraishis* 3:16.
43. Proverbs 12:4.
44. See Tosafos, *Zevachim* 103a.
45. [See also the subsection entitled The Woman's Unique Kiddush Hashem concerning trustworthiness.]
46. *Devarim* 19:15.
47. *Shmos* 19:6.
48. Psalms 45:14.
49. *Avos* 1:2.
50. See volume one of the *Hashkafa* Dialogue Series, "I Shall Not Want" the final chapter, *Sachar Limud.*
51. *Sota* 11b.
52. *Beraishis* 1:27.
53. *Yesodei HaTorah* 5:10. [Rambam is an acronym for Rabbi Moshe ben Maimon, otherwise known as Maimonides.]
54. Proverbs 20:27.
55. *Divrei HaYamim* II 11:2; see also *Melachim* (Kings) II:2.
56. [See subsection entitled Women and Groupings.]
57. [See section entitled Kiddush Hashem.]
58. [Rabbi Aryeh Kaplan wrote a fascinating pamphlet on the subject of *mikveh* called The Waters of Eden. See Appendix.]
59. *Shabbos* 62a.
60. *Ishus,* 15:20.
61. *Yevamos* 62b.
62. *Beraishis* 3:19.
63. *Beraishis* 3:16.
64. Commandment 16.
65. *Sota* 17a.

SHALHEVES

Information
and
Tape List

AUDIO TAPES
BY RABBI EZRIEL TAUBER

The following is a partial listing of tapes in English by Rabbi Ezriel Tauber, including lectures through the Fall of 5755. Also available are tapes in Hebrew, Yiddish, and Russian, as well as videos (see end of list). Prices are $4.00 per tape and $15.00 per video (plus shipping and handling). Visa and Mastercard accepted. For further information contact:

Shalheves
P.O. Box 361
Monsey, NY 10952
Phone: (914) 356-3515
Fax: (914) 425-2094

FOR BEGINNERS

75	Introductory Lecture To Non-Committed Jews
93	Business And Torah
146	For Beginners
165-A	The Creation And Its Purpose
165-B	The Creation And Its Purpose
167	Business And Torah
170	Life After Death
176	Is There Everyday Life?
201	Purpose Of Life (Part 1)
202	Mysticism In Everyday Life (Part 2)
203	Mysticism In Everyday Life (Part 3)
241	Who Am I?
250	New Times Of Teshuva
269	Should We Isolate Or Integrate?
295	Real Life
307	Jewish Concept Of Woman
316	The Structure Of The Jewish Nation
317	To Appreciate Our Role
323	Should We Plan?
338	The Value Of Time
354-A	Codes Revealed In The Torah
354-B	Codes Revealed In The Torah
394	The Definition Of "Yehudi"
757-A	Creation And Its Purpose
757-B	Creation And Its Purpose
758-A	Definition Of A Jewish Nation
758-B	The Benefit Of Suffering
759-A	Torah Concept Of Marriage
759-B	Torah Concept Of Marriage
796	Be A Proud Jew
817-A	Torah Concept Of Marriage
817-B	Reliance On Effort
818	The Value Of Life
855	Lets Represent G–D
872-A	Know G–D
872-B	Our Crucial Days
966-A	Codes In The Torah
966-B	Codes In The Torah
1003	The Meaning Of Happiness
1101	Destiny Of Life
1316	Appreciate Life
1341-A	Codes In The Torah
1341-B	Codes In The Torah
1431	You Can Be A Prophet
1452	Two Parts Of Life
1455	Are We Chosen?
1461	We, In Making Moshiach
1467	Only One Goal In Life
1489	To Live For Now
1497	We—As Hashem's Ambassadors
1502	A Life Which Is All Good
1506	Why Yaakov Tricks Eisav
1508	Yaakov Vs. Eisov
1511	The Real Reason For Anti-Semitism
1522	Questions And Answers
1532	Torah As A Map
1549	Mishpotim
1581	Avrohom—Today
1603	The Spies Of Today
1668	The Foundation Of Life
1671	Could A Holocaust Happen Without G–D?

AUDIO TAPES
BY RABBI EZRIEL TAUBER

INTERMEDIATE AND ADVANCED

EMUNAH & BITACHON

26	Thirteen Principles Of Faith
241	Who Am I?
782	Believing In Hashem
799	The Full Emunah
832	The First Principal Of Belief
1223	Believing
1292	Bitachon In Stressful Situations
1368	Applying Bitachon To Our Daily Struggles
1434	First Aid For Worriers
1445	Real Bitachon
1457	Finding Hashem When We Feel Alone
1541	The Need Of Bitachon Today
1565	Bitachon Is The Answer
1587	Money Covers Everything
1594	How To Practice Bitachon (Advanced)
1625	Belief In The Darkness
1645	The Definition Of Belief (8 tapes on The 13 Principles Of Faith; ask for album info.)
1654	Survival Today
1685	The Reality Of G–D
1686	Mitzvas Yichud Hashem
1693	How To Develop Faith
1695	Suffering Develops Faith
1696	Emunah In Practical Life
1700	Knowledge & Faith (included in the 8 tapes of The 13 Principles album; see 1645)

THE PURPOSE OF CREATION

144	The Tree Which Is A Fruit
518	The Purpose Of Creation
519	Yisroel—Fulfillment Of Creation
607	Life In Gan Eden
757-A	Creation And Its Purpose
757-B	Creation And Its Purpose
821-A	The Meaning Of Life
821-B	The Meaning Of Life
904-A	Creation And Its Purpose
904-B	Creation And Its Purpose
1098	Creation And Its Purpose

1338	A Time For Renewal
1438	Us In Creation
1586-A	The Jew And The World
1586-B	The Jew And The World
1722	The Process Of Creation

THE JEWISH NATION

269	Should We Isolate Or Integrate
648	The Jewish Nation's Responsibility To The World
758-A	Definition Of A Jewish Nation
758-B	The Benefit Of Suffering
805	My Share In The World To Come
872-A	Know G–D
872-B	Our Crucial Days
900	Let's Build Am Yisroel
901	Be Aware Of Your Duties
959	Leaving Egypt Today
1673	Live A Whole Life
1726	The Meaning Of Being Chosen

THE VALUE OF LIFE

903	Definition Of Truth And The Essence Of Life
997	Every Inch Of Life—Ongoing Bliss To Avodas Hashem
1000	The Value Of A Moment
1008	Every Moment A Mission To Hashem
1029	Is There Freedom Of Choice
1073	Positive Speech
1154	Value Of A Moment Of Life
1218	How To Grow Every Minute
1242	The Ultimate Goal
1243	The Real Free Choice
1315	Appreciate Life
1330	The Meaning Of Life
1340	Find Meaning In Life
1376	The Value Of Life
1682	The Value Of Life
1704	The Value Of Life

THE MEANING OF A JEW

640	Live With Confidence
690	Effort Of Competition

AUDIO TAPES
BY RABBI EZRIEL TAUBER

AUDIO TAPES
BY RABBI EZRIEL TAUBER

TESHUVA

188	Our Responsibility Towards The World
250	New Time Of Teshuva
258-A	The Teshuva Prophecy Realized
258-B	The Teshuva Prophecy Realized

TEFILLAH

772	An Effective Prayer
1102	Depth Of Tefillah
1551	The Power Of Tefillah
1558	How To Pray
1595	How Prayer Works (Part 1) (Advanced)
1596	How Prayer Works (Part 2) (Advanced)

LASHON HORAH

837	I, As A Messenger
1240	Why Loshon Horah?

CHINUCH

101	A Lecture To Teachers Of Girls
740	"Chinuch"—The Real Way
960	When Children Question Our Values
1006-A	Chinuch—The Courage To Say No
1006-B	Chinuch—The Courage To Say No
1014	Chinuch For Yourself
1030	The Right Chinuch
1031	Chinuch And Tznius
1590	Parents As Role Models
1599	The Method Of Education
1698	The Parents' Role In Finding The Right Shidduch
1707	The Challenge Of Raising Young Adults
1717	The Final Solution Or Resolution?

MARRIAGE

759-A	Torah Concept Of Marriage
759-B	Torah Concept Of Marriage
1209	Harmony In The Home (Part 1)
1210	Harmony In The Home (Part 2)
1236	How Marriage Helps Us Realize Our Potential
1440	The Torah Concept Of Marriage
1512	For Kallahs
1655	The Foundation Of Marriage
1699	Lecture To Kallahs

FOR MEN

618	The Man's Role In A Jewish Family
1080	Lecture For Chassanim (5 Parts—A-E)
1550	Man's Role In Marriage
1559	For Men Only
1597	The Man's Role In Marriage

FOR WOMEN

100	In The Merit Of Righteous Women We Were Redeemed..
546	Kidush Hashem By Women
613	The Woman's Role In The Family
620	"Man And Woman He Created Them"
623	The Woman's Role In Judaism
625	A Happy Jewish Family
651	Woman's Role In Building The Bais Hamikdash
1087	Lecture For Kallahs
1296	The Meaning Of Marriage
1304	The Woman's Role In Marriage
1598	The Woman's Role In Marriage

FOR GIRLS

108	For A Girl—Leaving Egypt
709	Role Of A Jewish Girl
845	Let's Care For Each Other (The 3 Weeks)
1057	My Role In Creation
1135	Appreciate Being Chosen
1374	For The Seminary Girl
1702	Chessed Of A Bas Yisroel

AUDIO TAPES
BY RABBI EZRIEL TAUBER

PARSHA

80	Parshas Bereishis
1493	The Man As A Tree (Bereishis)
1286	The Significance Of The Binding Of Yizchok (Vayaira)
1283	Know Who You Are (Vayaira)
1495	Akaidas Yitzchok Today (Vayaira)
1288	Sarah's Life, All Good (Chayai Sara)
921	Yaakov's Purchase Of Esav's Bechorah (Toldos)
1509	How To Ask Hashem (Toldos)
153	Parshas Vayeitsei
95	Parshas Vayechi
168	Be Like Ephraim And Menasha (Vayechi)
635	The Bush Burning In Fire (Va'Ara)
119	Parshas Yisro-Mishpotim
1556	Build Me A Sanctuary (Truma)
192	Make Your Own Luchos (Ki Sisa)
1564	Half Shekel Or Golden Calf (Ki Sisa)
195	Women's Participation In Building Of The Mishkan (Pekudai)
666	Benefits Of The Jewish Dietary Laws (Shmini)
695	Parshas Hameraglim (Shlach)
1602	No Reason To Fear (Shlach)
1605	The Only Medicine Today (Shlach)
1608	Parshas Shlach
1611	Not To Be Like Korach—Today
1614	Parshas Chukas
245	Listen And Then Realize (R'ah)

MISCELLANEOUS

266	The Role Of Our Mother Rachel
517-A	The Definition Of Truth
517-B	The Definition Of Truth
557	Should We Be Exposed To The World

630	Fashion—The Uniform Of A Goy
632	Multiple Plans In The Universe
752	Love Hashem
755	Curiosity—Why?
787	To Combat Proudness
833	One Solution For All Problems
840	Live For The Present
847	Discover Your Wisdom
851	Questions And Answers
857	The Meaning Of Chessed
863	Tranquility
907	Prophecies In Our Times
915	Questions And Answers
927	Money As Eternity
944	We As Survivors
948	Develop The Right Desire
964	You Cannot Dilute The Truth
966-A	Codes In The Torah
966-B	Codes In The Torah
967	Prophecies Materialized In Our Times
1021	Achievements Of Positive Thinking
1094	Getting Things Done
1097	The Definition Of Truth
1148	Honoring Parents
1185	Questions & Answers
1187	Justify Your Consumption
1190	Questions & Answers
1211	Remembering
1321	How To Find A Friend
1341-A	Codes In The Torah
1341-B	Codes In The Torah
1412	Think Right
1449	Thoughtfulness—Patch Of Relationships
1451	Let's Start Thinking
1460	Free Will Vs. Fate
1520	Three Conditions To Chassidus
1527	How To Acquire Chassidus
1542	The Ladder Of Shovevim
1543	Holocaust And Zionism
1544	Learning The Truth From Falsehood
1545	Chizuk
1546	The Importance Of Unity
1580	Self Discover Truth
1592	Find Your Greatness In Your Nothingness

AUDIO TAPES
BY RABBI EZRIEL TAUBER

AUDIO TAPES
BY RABBI EZRIEL TAUBER

132	Mechanics Of Teshuva
135	Real Chessed
136	Teshuva With Simcha
249	Teshuva With Shofar
261	My Only Request Of Hashem
446	Be An Original Jew
600	Meaning Of The Akaidah
711	Fill In Your Time
719	Obtaining Love Of Hashem
720	Choose Life
862	Truth
864	In The Book Of Life
1033	The Advantage Of Elul
1039	The Concealed Power In You
1048	My Resolution
1265	A Full Jew
1470	What Is There For Us To Give?
1472	What Are We Giving To Hashem?
1643	Elul

ROSH HASHANNAH

718	Two Ways Of Praying
867	What Can I Give To Hashem?
869	Let's Be Honest
876	Corronate Hashem
878	Make Me King
1034	Let's Corronate Hashem
1035	I, As A Representative Of Hashem
1055	Power Of Prayer
1259	Please Corronate Me
1642	The Gift Of Rosh Hashono

YOM KIPPUR

722	Take Yom Kippur With You
881	Join Me Totally
883	Do It For Your Name
1061	The Mitzvah In Teshuva
1480	I Am Ready For Trial
1482	Corronate Me
1483	Chessed, All The Time
1647	My Real Identity
1650	Let's Thank Hashem

SUCCOS

603	Decoration To G–D
890	The Meaning Of Simcha

894	The Real Truth

CHANUKAH

161	The Eternal Light
271	Chanuka, 5745
746	Bring Chanukah
920	Why Are We Hated
926	Me As Hashem's Candle
935	Mizvas Yediah—Emunah
939	Me As A Chanukah-Light
1295	The Four Goluses
1306	Surprises About Chanukah
1310	Bayomim Hohaim Bizman Hazeh
1515	Chanuka
1518	Self Esteem
1690	Kindle Your Own Flame
1691	To Thank And To Praise

PURIM

105	How To Oppose Amalek And Pharaoh
777	Fight Amalek
779	Develop Simcha
784	Enjoying The Golus
792	The Homon Of Today
793	Mordechai And Esther Today
797	Egypt In Our Times
971	How To Generate Simcha
972	Assimilating Whilst Religious
974	Pesach—Purim—Pesach
1159	How Is Amalek Effecting Us
1344	A Successful Simcha
1359	Revelation Of Yisroel
1377	Opportunities You Might Miss
1557	Pharaoh-Amalek/Purim-Pesach
1561	Getting Rid Of Amalek
1562	The End Of Amalek
1719	How To Develop Simcha
1720	Simcha Against Amalek

TAPE SERIES

Chovas Halevavos (100 Tapes)
Maharal—Netzach Yisroel (53 Tapes)
Maharal—Nesiv Hateshuva (18 Tapes)
Maharal—Gevuros Hashem (100 Tapes, more upcoming)
Maharal—On The Haggadah (15 Tapes)
Maharal—Rosh Hashannah (3 Tapes)

AUDIO TAPES
BY RABBI EZRIEL TAUBER

Maharal—Ohr Chodosh (3 Tapes)
Ramchal—Daas Tevunos (73 Tapes)
Ramchal—Derech Hashem (7 Tapes)
Ramchal—Mesilas Yeshorim (62 Tapes)
Tefillah (4 Tapes)
Shir Hashirim (12 Tapes)
Koheles (29 Tapes)
Tanya (52 Tapes)
Series Of Tapes For Chassanim (5 Tapes)
Series Of Tapes For Kallahs—Various
    Speakers (6 Tapes)

TAPE SERIES FOR SPECIAL GROUPS

Series Of Lectures For Divorcees
Series Of Lectures For Childless Couples
Series Of Lectures For Single Girls
Series Of Lectures For Widows
Series Of Lectures For Bereaved Parents

YIDDISH

Chovos Halevavos (51 Tapes)
Tanya (30 Tapes)
Bechol Derochechah Daihu (10 Tapes)
Series Of Tapes For Chassanim (5 Tapes)
Ramchal—Mesilas Yeshorim (8 Tapes)
Ramchal—Derech Hashem (12 Tapes)
Maharal—Tiferes Yisroel (52 Tapes)
Maharal—Netzach Yisroel (25 Tapes)
Maharal—Derech Chaim (19 Tapes)
Maharal—Gevuros Hashem (14 Tapes)
Maharal—Nesiv Hatorah (9 Tapes)

HEBREW

Chovos Helevavos (86 Tapes)

Parshas Hashovua (81 Tapes)
Shir Hashirim (7 Tapes)
Tefillah (30 Tapes)
Ramchal—Mesilas Yeshorim (25 Tapes)
Ramchal—Mamar Haikrim (6 Tapes)
Ramchal—Derech Etz Chaim (7 Tapes)

VIDEOS

1. Hidden Codes In The Torah
2. Soul Searching (With Dr. Brian Weiss)
3. The Definition Of Truth
4. Creation And Its Purpose
5. Definition Of Life
6. Torah Concept Of Marriage
7. Harmony And Peace In The Jewish Home
8. "Golus"—The Benefit Of Suffering
9. Panel Discussion—Questions And Answers
10. The Significance Of Torah And Tefillah
11. The Meaning Of Shabbos
12. Prophecies Materialized In Our Times
13. Effort And Bitachon Towards Making A Living
14. Improving
15. Practicality In Day To Day Life
16. Choose Life
17. "We Are One"—Why And How
18. Us In Creation
19. Tranquility In Business

BOOKS

In today's times of stress and spiritual alienation, everyone feels a void somewhere in his or her life. Whether beginner or advanced scholar, the books of Rabbi Ezriel Tauber have helped people fill their voids. A survivor of the Holocaust, Rabbi Tauber's method—backed by years as a teacher and counselor—emphasizes the importance of learning to help oneself. Marriage, finances, doubts—his books cover the gamut of life's experiences and help you become your own psychologist and spiritual guide.

Self Esteem

Self-Esteem is a treasure map to the self. More than a manual of ideas on feeling good about oneself, it is the personal account of four different adults (based on true case histories) whose difficulties in life have negated their feelings of self-worth, making them anxious and unhappy. **Self-Esteem** will give you both the inspiration to undertake that epic journey to the center of yourself, as well as the practical advice how to stay on course during the often stormy days and nights of that journey.

(284 Pages)

Choose Life!

Choose Life! is an impact book. David, a 30-year-old professional, found out he had cancer and was so depressed that he decided not to take the chemotherapy that could save him. Reading **Choose Life!** changed his entire outlook and he decided to undergo the therapy with renewed courage. **Choose Life!** delivers . . . Rabbi Tauber shows us how to find ultimate meaning in our lives. Whether for yourself or a friend, choosing **Choose Life!** is a choice you will not regret.

(238 Pages)

Beyond Survival

Beyond Survival is based on the famous Thirteen Principles of Maimonides. However, whereas most scholars expound on the Thirteen Principles to teach the basic tenets of Jewish faith, Rabbi Tauber goes beyond that and shows how each principle is a vital tool for spiritual growth and personal development. For instance,

- belief in the Creator's oneness is the foundation of self-esteem
- understanding what it means to believe in the coming of the Messiah is the psychological cornerstone for conquering adversity
- knowing that your body will come back to life will revolutionize the way you think of your physical self and surroundings.

Understood properly, the Thirteen Principles will naturally produce a penetrating, soulful outlook on life which helps you deal with the most difficult and confusing situations you find yourself in—be they family relationships, raising children, making a living, surviving a crisis, etc. In many ways the most inclusive of Rabbi Tauber's books, **Beyond Survival** is sure to help you turn every life experience and difficulty into a self-replenishing wellspring of renewal and growth.

(177 Pages)

BOOKS
BY RABBI EZRIEL TAUBER

Darkness Before Dawn

Darkness Before Dawn is a book about how to grow from adversity. Proceeding with the assumption that the community is simply a larger version of the individual, it discusses the reasons behind the long history of Jewish suffering. Ultimately, the tragedy of the Holocaust is discussed. The end result is a document which helps each of us grapple with and overcome the personal holocaust we may be suffering. As a survivor of the Holocaust, the book is central to Rabbi Tauber's entire outlook and includes some of his most personal, gripping, and profound words. No one is immune to the trials and tribulations of suffering. No one. Yet, the darkest part of the night is the moment just before dawn. Help yourself or someone you know learn to grow from hardship and tragedy.

(274 Pages)

I Shall Not Want

I Shall Not Want: The Torah Outlook on Working for a Living delves into the simple yet profound message of faith. At the same time, it endeavors to show how pursuit of career and financial gain need not be a contradiction to faith. Indeed, in the Jewish perspective, each potentially enhances the other. True inner peace should not be dependent upon economic peaks and valleys. **I Shall Not Want** can help you attain the peace of mind necessary to pass unscathed through your personal valley overshadowed by death.

(134 Pages)

To Become One

To Become One: The Torah Outlook on Marriage "should be required reading for a couple about to be married and for many that are already married," writes a major Jewish periodical. Drawn from over three decades of counseling experience, Rabbi Tauber presents the deep underpinnings of the most profound of human relationships and includes a plethora of practical strategies for side-stepping or resolving conflicts. His formula for successful marriage has helped marriages of all types, even ones that were unhappy for over twenty years! Whether you are happily married, unhappily married, or just thinking about marriage, this book supplies the basic tools that can help you become one with your spouse.

(180 Pages)

Days Are Coming

Days Are Coming is a fascinating dialogue between a rabbi, an atheistic Israeli Zionist, and a searching American collegiate. More than just good entertainment, it is designed to help you feel in greater control of the ominous and foreboding events happening in our days. We have no need to be reminded of the upheavals occurring all over the world. Some believe them to be heralds of a new age. Others are confused and fearful, and only see in them the ugly face of fanaticism. The Jewish world, too, has undergone major upheavals. Do they portend good or bad? Is there something we can do about it? Read **Days Are Coming**.

(226 Pages)